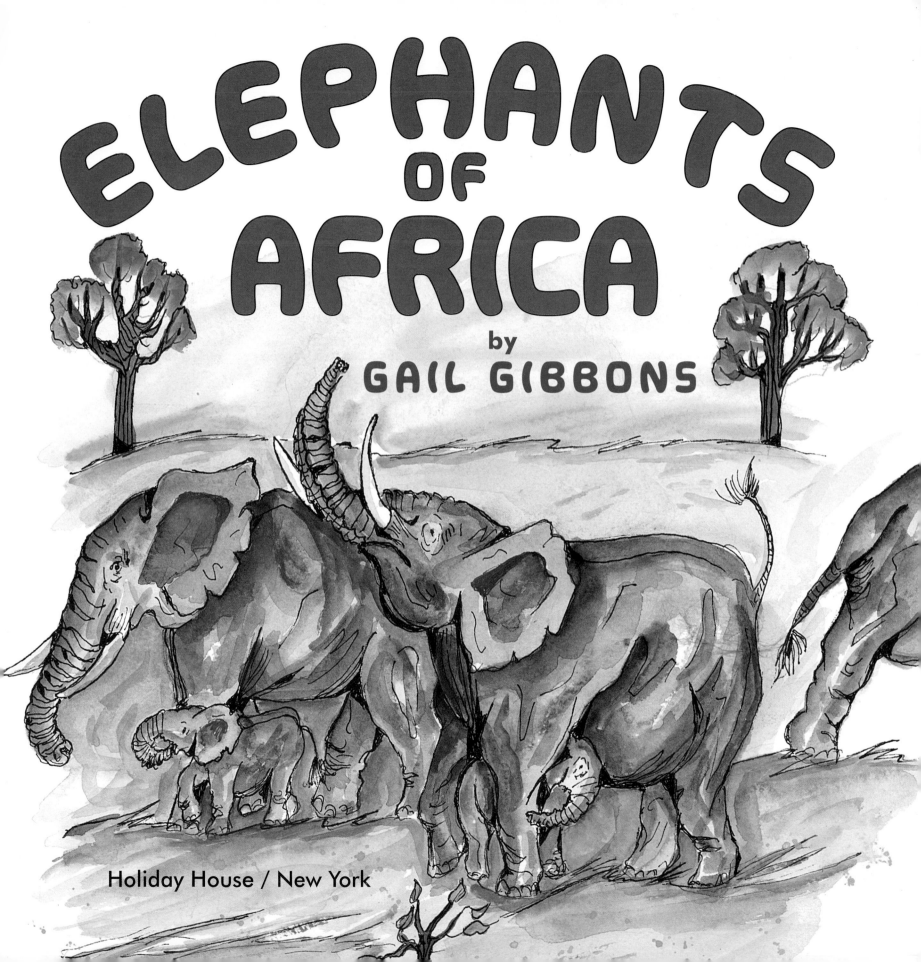

ELEPHANTS OF AFRICA

by
GAIL GIBBONS

Holiday House / New York

To Lorenzo Buttignol

Special thanks to Jim Doherty,
General Curator Emeritus of the New York Zoological Society,
Bronx, New York.

Library of Congress Cataloging-in-Publication Data
Gibbons, Gail.
Elephants of Africa / by Gail Gibbons. — 1st ed.
p. cm.
ISBN 978-0-8234-2168-8 (hardcover)
1. Elephants—Juvenile literature. I. Title.
QL737.P98G53 2008
599.67—dc22
2007051619

A SAVANNA is a large grassland with scattered trees.

A HERD is a group of the same kind of animals.

A herd of African elephants makes its way across the vast savanna. Elephants are the largest living land animals.

African elephants also live in forests.

4

AREAS IN AFRICA WHERE MOST ELEPHANTS LIVE

AFRICA

ATLANTIC OCEAN

INDIAN OCEAN

MASTODON

MAMMOTH

Thousands of years ago there were about 350 different kinds of elephants. The mammoth and the mastodon were prehistoric members of the elephant family. They had thick fur to protect them from the cold.

AFRICAN ELEPHANT CHARACTERISTICS

ARCHED BACK

LARGE EARS

FLAT FOREHEAD

EYE

TRUNK

NECK

MOUTH

TUSKS

Two "FINGERS" at end of trunk

THICK LEGS

TAIL with thick hair at end

PADDED FEET

TOENAILS

A male African elephant can grow to be 13 feet (3.9 meters) tall and weigh as much as 7 tons (6.3 metric tons). Females are smaller and weigh about 5 tons (4.5 metric tons).

AN ELEPHANT'S TRUNK

The trunk has thousands of muscles. The "fingers" at the end of the trunk are so sensitive that they can pick a leaf off a tree.

BREATHING

SMELLING

DRINKING

The trunk of an elephant is a combination of its nose and its upper lip. It is strong and flexible, and has many uses.

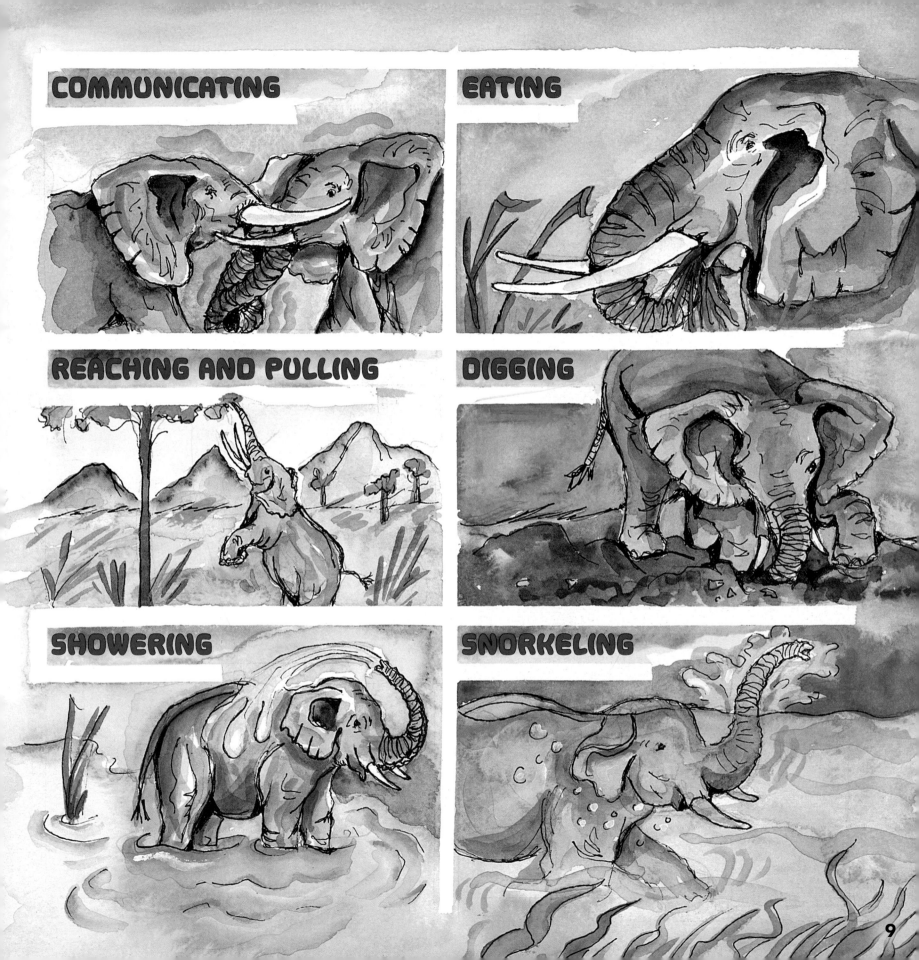

COMMUNICATING

EATING

REACHING AND PULLING

DIGGING

SHOWERING

SNORKELING

9

AN ELEPHANT'S TUSKS

TUSKS

STRIPPING OFF BARK FOR FOOD

DIGGING FOR WATER

DIGGING UP ROOTS FOR FOOD

Tusks are large teeth that grow out of each side of the upper jaw. An elephant uses its tusks in many different ways.

DEFENDING THEIR YOUNG

MALES BATTLING OVER A POSSIBLE MATE

Tusks start to grow when an elephant is very young and continue to grow throughout its life. They can be as long as 13 feet (3.9 meters) and weigh as much as 200 pounds (90.7 kilograms).

AN ELEPHANT'S SKIN

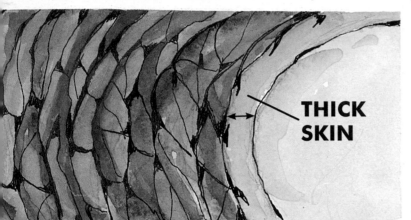

THICK SKIN

Most of the skin of an elephant is about 1.5 inches (3.8 centimeters) thick to protect the elephant from its harsh environment. When it is very hot elephants roll and wallow in mud and blow sand or soil over their backs to form mud packs. This protects their skin from sunburn and helps keep their bodies cooler.

The end of a TAIL has coarse hairs up to 30 inches (76.2 centimeters) long.

To help protect their sensitive skin from flies and other biting insects, elephants will shower themselves with water, sand, or soil. They may also use their tails to swat away these pests.

AN ELEPHANT'S EARS

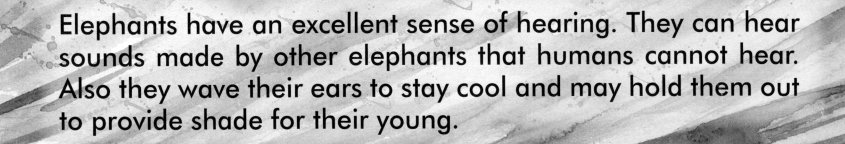

Elephants have an excellent sense of hearing. They can hear sounds made by other elephants that humans cannot hear. Also they wave their ears to stay cool and may hold them out to provide shade for their young.

AN ELEPHANT'S EYES

Elephants have poor eyesight. In bright sunlight they can only see clearly up to about 60 feet (18.3 meters). Elephants see better when the light is not bright. Good hearing and a good sense of smell help make up for poor vision.

AN ELEPHANT'S TEETH

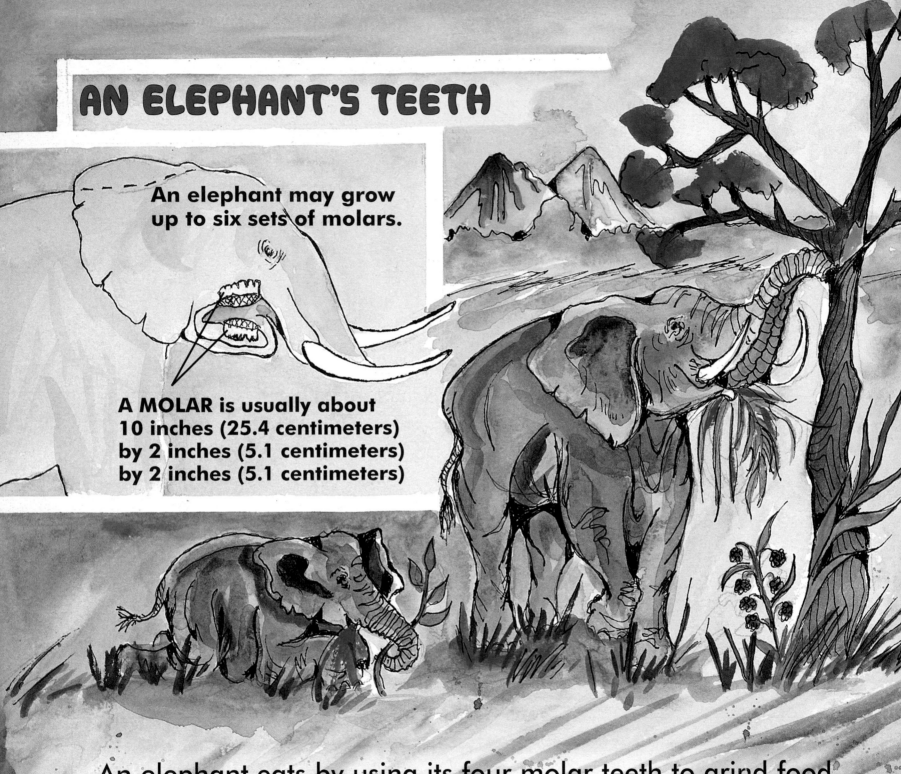

An elephant may grow up to six sets of molars.

A MOLAR is usually about 10 inches (25.4 centimeters) by 2 inches (5.1 centimeters) by 2 inches (5.1 centimeters)

An elephant eats by using its four molar teeth to grind food. Elephants in the wild may eat more than 300 pounds (136 kilograms) of food in a day. They eat branches, grasses, leaves, bark, roots, fruits, and berries.

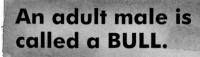

An adult male is called a BULL.

With gentle reassurance, a mother helps her calf stand up on its feet.

An adult female is called a COW.

A CALF usually weighs 250 pounds (113.4 kilograms) and stands about 3 feet (.9 meter) tall at birth.

A baby elephant is called a CALF.

When it is mating time males may compete for the attention of a female. The females usually mate every four to five years. About 22 months after mating the female gives birth.

For about two years the young calf will need to drink gallons of its mother's milk every day. At two years old, it will continue to nurse plus begin to eat leaves and other grown-up foods that its mother is eating. At about four or five years old it will be completely weaned off its mother's milk.

On rare occasions, family groups may include adopted orphans.

Elephants are social animals and live in family groups of about six to twelve elephants. The adults are all females, usually a mother and her daughters. The rest are their calves of varying ages. The members of the group stay together.

19

Young male elephants joust and play with one another, learning how to defend themselves when they go out on their own. They usually leave the family group at about ten years of age and live with other young bull elephants.

By the age of twenty-five to thirty-five years old, a bull elephant is likely to be living on its own, but usually not far from family groups.

Females stay with their family group and help to raise the young. When the group gets too big, one or two adult females, usually sisters, go off with their calves. Together they start a new family group.

The family group is led by a matriarch, usually the eldest and most experienced female. She knows her home range, how to find food and water, and how to avoid enemies.

FINDING FOOD

Elephants are always on the move looking for food. The matriarch knows when and where to find favorite or abundant food and water. The elephants spread out and the younger ones learn their survival skills by watching and imitating their mother and the older elephants in the group.

Elephants have been known to carry food to old or sickly elephants that are unable to forage on their own.

Elephants spend most of the day and night feeding or looking for their next meal.

Elephants don't like to be separated from one another. When they come back together, they greet one another by flapping their ears, making screeching and trumpeting sounds, and winding their trunks together with affection.

When the food in the area is gone, family groups may join together and form a herd. They move on.

FINDING WATER

An elephant sucks up about 2 gallons (7.6 liters) of water into its trunk and then blows the water into its mouth. It may drink about 40 gallons (151.4 liters) a day.

Young ones squeal as they fill their trunks and squirt each other.

They wallow in the mud to stay cool. This protects them from the sun and annoying insects.

Elephants need a lot of water.

When water is not readily available, the matriarch is said to be able to smell water under the ground miles away. She will use her tusks and front feet to dig down into the earth, starting a watering hole. This will benefit other animals as well.

The elephants make loud trumpeting sounds.

They spread their ears to make themselves look bigger.

They gather around the young ones to protect them.

Other than humans, elephants' only enemies are hyenas and lions, which have been known to kill baby elephants. The scent of a lion or hyena strikes fear in all elephants. If they can't get away, the whole group will do what is necessary to keep the calves safe.

POACHERS are people who hunt illegally. With elephants they normally just poach to take the ivory tusks. Don't buy elephant ivory!

PRESERVE

Elephants are threatened by expanding human settlements and by poachers. Nature preserves have been created. Wardens are there to help protect the elephants from poachers. These special animals deserve respect and consideration.

ELEPHANT TRACKS

Elephants are found in warm climates. They don't have a layer of fat to protect them from freezing temperatures.

Elephants can walk very quietly because they have thick pads on the bottoms of their feet.

In the wild, elephants may live to be more than sixty years old.

An elephant can move as fast as 18 to 25 miles per hour (28.9 kilometers to 40.2 kilometers).

Elephants usually sleep standing up for about three to four hours a day.

Elephants can swim for hours and go several miles.

Ninety-nine percent of baby elephants are born at night.

GOODNIGHT MOON

by Margaret Wise Brown
Pictures by Clement Hurd

In the great green room
There was a telephone
And a red balloon
And a picture of—

The cow jumping over the moon

And there were three little bears sitting on chairs

And two little kittens
And a pair of mittens

And a little toyhouse
And a young mouse

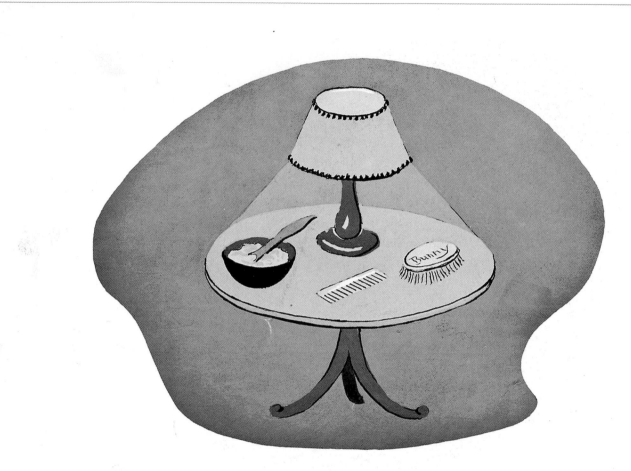

And a comb and a brush and a bowl full of mush

And a quiet old lady who was whispering "hush"

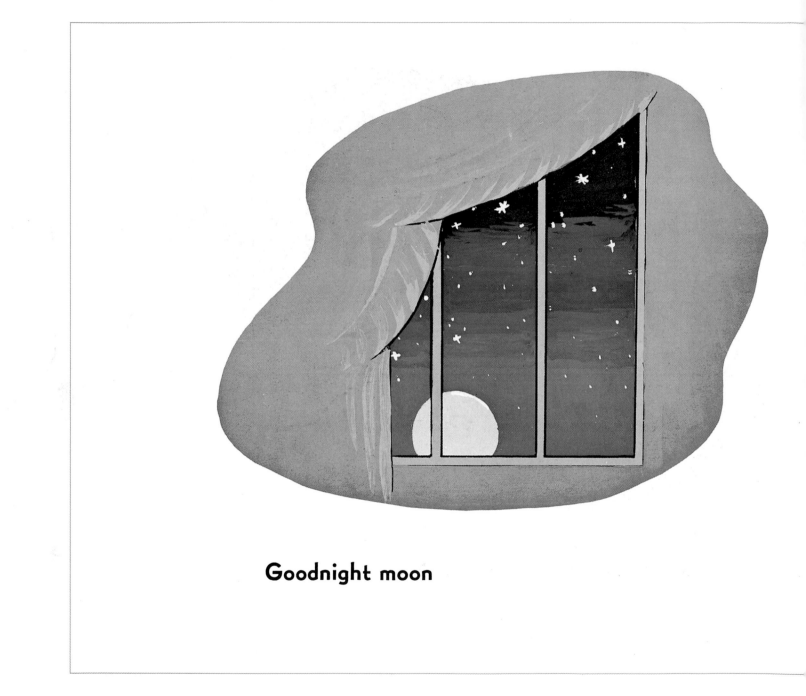

Goodnight moon

Goodnight cow jumping over the moon

Goodnight light
And the red balloon

Goodnight bears
Goodnight chairs

Goodnight kittens

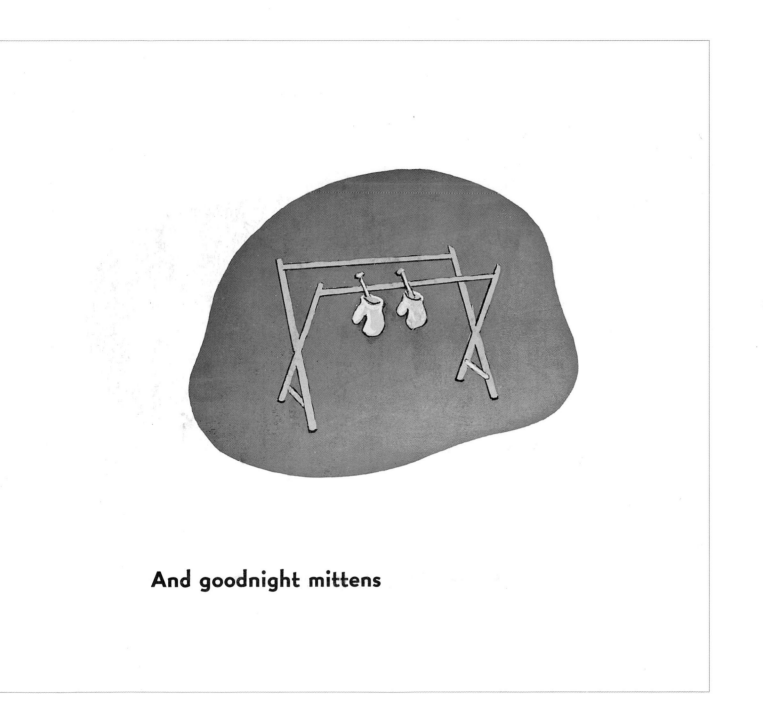

And goodnight mittens

Goodnight clocks
And goodnight socks

Goodnight little house

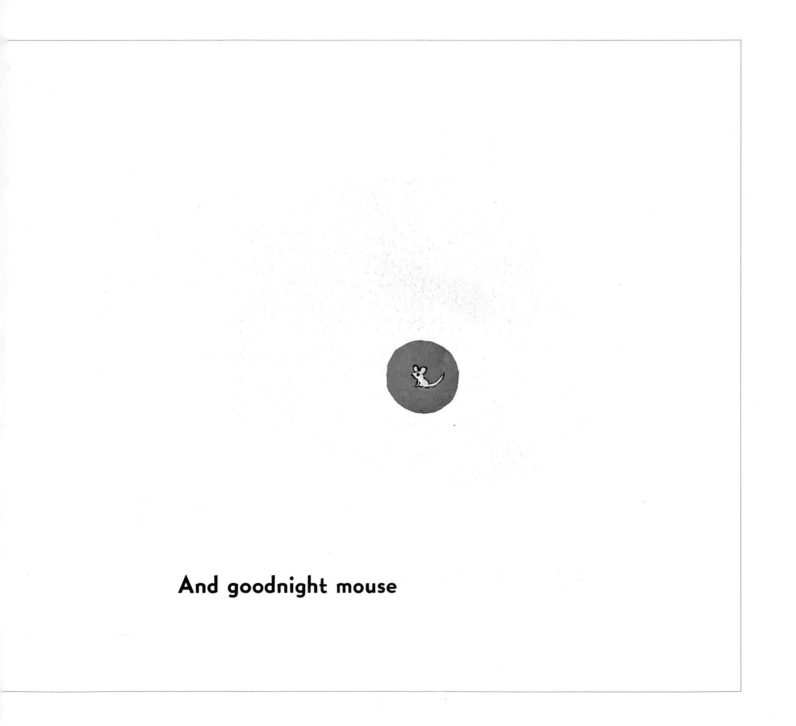

And goodnight mouse

Goodnight comb
And goodnight brush

Goodnight nobody

Goodnight mush

And goodnight to the old lady
whispering "hush"

43

Goodnight stars

Goodnight air

Goodnight noises everywhere

GOODNIGHT MOON

1947

Goodnight noises everywhere

When *Goodnight Moon* is read aloud, it takes on the quality of a classic lullaby, as though it has been around for centuries. And because the lullaby works, parents never tire of reading *Goodnight Moon* over and over again.

The appeal of Clement Hurd's artwork lies in its combined mystery and graphic simplicity. The great green room is inexhaustible for children; they can search for each object again and again, and feel the changes in the room as the night descends throughout the book.

How to enjoy *Goodnight Moon* further:
+ Search for the mouse—he's in a different spot on each page.
+ Point out the different objects in the room and ask your child to name them.
+ Have your child draw a picture of his or her own room and identify different objects.
+ Create your own bedtime ritual—which could include reading *Goodnight Moon.*

Margaret Wise Brown (1910–1952) was a unique personality in the world of children's books—flamboyant, quirky, and glamorous. Born in New York City and educated at Hollins College, she began her work as a writer for children after studying at the Bureau of Educational Experiments in New York, also known as "Bank Street." At Bank Street, she was mentored by Lucy Sprague Mitchell, whose progressive theories about preschool children and their development helped shape Brown's work as a writer, and also as an editor for the publisher William R. Scott. During her tragically short career, she created more than one hundred deceptively simple stories that reflected a preschool child's inner fantasy life as well as his or her outer reality, and that were strikingly poetic and musical.

Clement Hurd (1908–1988) graduated from Yale University and studied painting in Paris. He was encouraged by Margaret Wise Brown to try picture book illustration, and many of his works are now considered the most popular books ever published for children. They include *Goodnight Moon, The Runaway Bunny,* and *My World* by Margaret Wise Brown, and more than forty books authored by his wife, Edith Thacher. With his bold, colorful compositions, he illustrated over seventy books during his career.

CAPS
FOR SALE

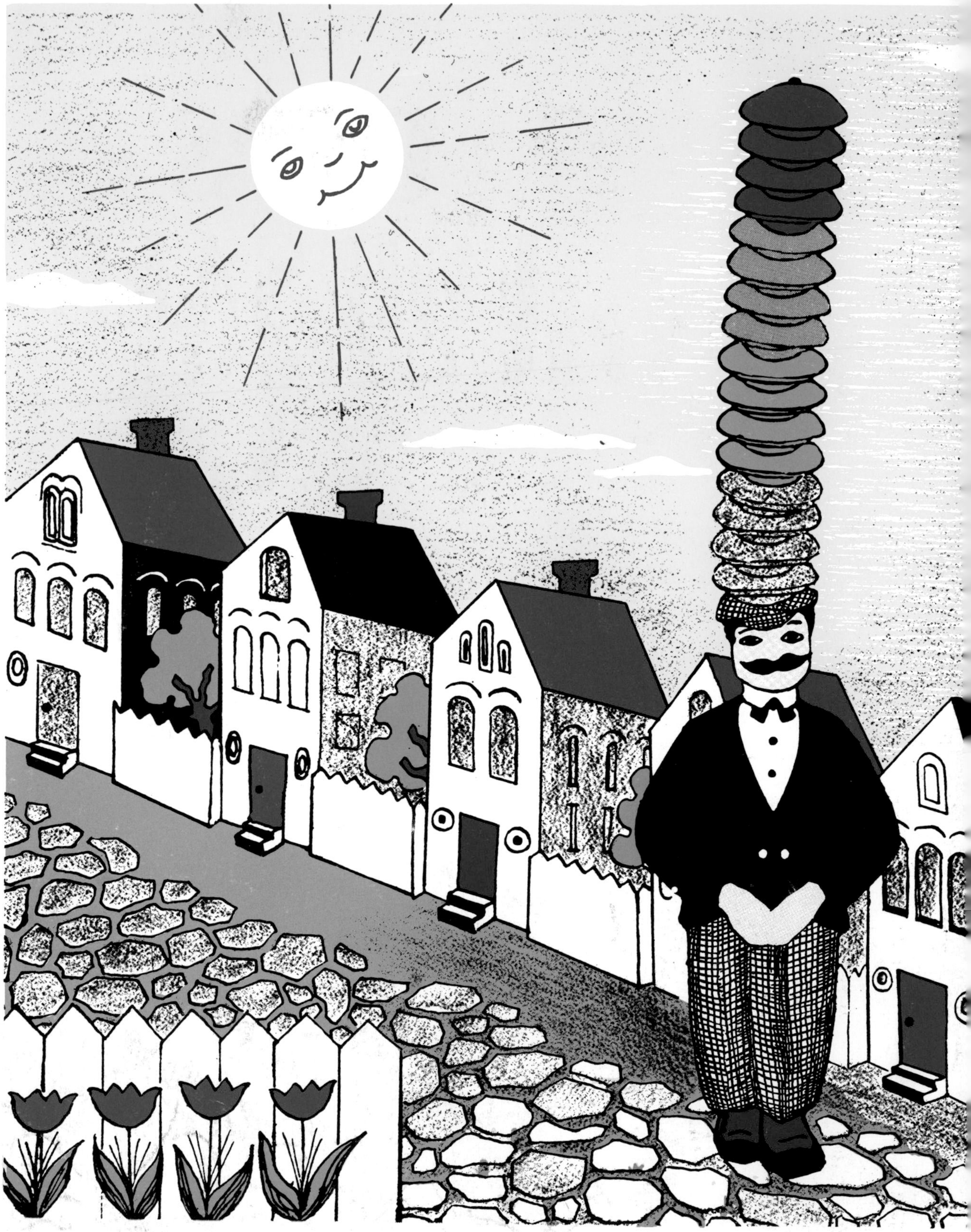

CAPS
FOR SALE

A Tale of a Peddler, Some Monkeys
and Their Monkey Business

Told and Illustrated by

Esphyr Slobodkina

To Rosalind and Emmy Jean,
and to their grandfather
who loved to read to them

54

Once there was
a peddler who sold caps.
But he was not like
an ordinary peddler
carrying his wares on his back.
He carried them
on top of his head.

First he had on his own
checked cap,
then a bunch of gray caps,
then a bunch of brown caps,
then a bunch of blue caps,
and on the very top
a bunch of red caps.

He walked
up and down the streets,
holding himself very straight
so as not to upset his caps.

As he went along he called,
"Caps! Caps for sale!
Fifty cents a cap!"

58

One morning

he couldn't sell any caps.

He walked up the street and

he walked down the street calling,

"Caps! Caps for sale. Fifty cents a cap."

But nobody wanted any caps

that morning.

Nobody wanted even a red cap.

He began to feel very hungry,

but he had no money for lunch.

"I think I'll go for a walk in the country,"

said he.

And he walked out of town—

slowly, slowly,

so as not to upset his caps.

He walked for a long time
until he came to a great big tree.

"That's a nice place for a rest,"
thought he.

And he sat down very slowly, under the tree
and leaned back little by little
against the tree-trunk so as not to disturb
the caps on his head.

Then he put up his hand to feel
if they were straight—
first his own checked cap,
then the gray caps,
then the brown caps,
then the blue caps,
then the red caps
on the very top.

They were all there.

So he went to sleep.

He slept for a long time.

When he woke up
he was refreshed
and rested.

But before standing up
he felt with his hand
to make sure his caps were
in the right place.

All he felt was his own
checked cap!

He looked to the right of him.
No caps.

He looked to the left of him.
No caps.

He looked in back of him.
No caps.

He looked behind the tree.
No caps.

Then he looked up into the tree.

And what do you think he saw?

On every branch sat a monkey. On every monkey

was a gray, or a brown, or a blue, or a red cap!

The peddler looked
at the monkeys.

The monkeys looked
at the peddler.

He didn't know
what to do.

Finally he spoke to them.

"You monkeys, you,"
he said,
shaking a finger at them,
"you give me back my caps."

But the monkeys
only shook their fingers
back at him and said,
"Tsz, tsz, tsz."

This made the peddler angry,
so he shook both hands
at them and said,
"You monkeys, you!
You give me back my caps."

But the monkeys only
shook both their hands
back at him and said,
"Tsz, tsz, tsz."

Now he felt quite angry.

He stamped his foot,

and he said,

"You monkeys, you!

You better give me back my caps!"

But the monkeys only

stamped their feet

back at him and said,

"Tsz, tsz, tsz."

By this time
the peddler was really
very, very angry.
He stamped both his feet and
shouted, "You monkeys, you!
You must give me back my caps!"

But the monkeys only
stamped both their feet
back at him and said,
"Tsz, tsz, tsz."

At last he became
so angry that he
pulled off his own cap,
threw it on the ground, and
began to walk away.

But then,
each monkey
pulled off
his cap . . .

and all the gray caps,

and all the brown caps,

and all the blue caps,

and all the red caps

came flying down

out of the tree.

So the peddler
picked up his caps and
put them back on his head—

first his own checked cap,

then the gray caps,

then the brown caps,

then the blue caps,

then the red caps
on the very top.

And slowly, slowly,

he walked back to town calling,

"Caps! Caps for sale!

Fifty cents a cap!"

CAPS FOR SALE

A Tale of a Peddler, Some Monkeys and Their Monkey Business

1947

"You monkeys, you! You give me back my caps."

Repetition and humor make *Caps for Sale* a great read-aloud experience. Children love to engage in the furor of the peddler and the antics of the monkeys and delight in mimicking the *tsz, tsz, tsz* sounds. Decades after its first publication, *Caps for Sale* continues to enrapture preschool audiences.

Esphyr Slobodkina, like many illustrators of the time, worked in three colors, although her choices—turquoise blue, red, and ochre—were quite unusual. When she was researching the story, based on a folktale, of *Caps for Sale*, she came to the conclusion that the only place it could have originated was Paramaribo, a Dutch colony at the tip of South America. Upon visiting Paramaribo, Slobodkina was struck by the odd combination of prim Dutch architecture and a lively monkey population.

How to enjoy *Caps for Sale* further:

+ Pretend you are a monkey! What kind of noises do you make? How do you act?
+ Act out the story with your child. What does "monkey see, monkey do" mean?
+ The peddler sorts his caps according to their color—gray, brown, blue, and red. Cut hat shapes out of different-colored felt or paper and let your child place them on a doll's head. Sort the caps according to their color and show how the caps can be arranged in different sequences.

Esphyr Slobodkina—painter, writer, sculptor, interior decorator, and illustrator—was born in 1908 in Siberia, Russia, and immigrated to the United States in 1928. Her many books for children are often based on folklore, and her simply told stories are filled with repetition and action. Her work is a part of the fabric of twentieth-century modern art and is represented in the Smithsonian and New York City's Metropolitan and Whitney museums. Slobodkina collaborated with Margaret Wise Brown on her first book for children, *The Little Fireman,* published by William R. Scott. Scott was also the original publisher of *Caps for Sale* (Harper & Row acquired the publishing rights from another publishing company that had acquired the Scott backlist). Many of Slobodkina's other works, including *Circus Caps for Sale* and *The Wonderful Feast,* are still in print years after publication.

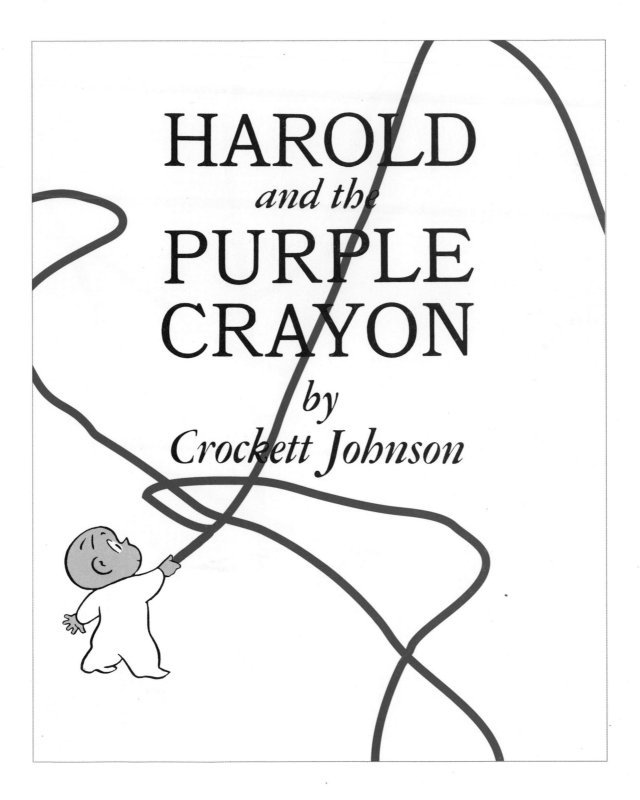

HAROLD
and the
PURPLE CRAYON

by

Crockett Johnson

One evening, after thinking it over for
some time, Harold decided to go for a walk
in the moonlight.

There wasn't any moon, and Harold needed a
moon for a walk in the moonlight.

And he needed something to walk on.

He made a long straight path so he wouldn't get lost.

And he set off on his walk, taking his big
purple crayon with him.

But he didn't seem to be getting anywhere
on the long straight path.

So he left the path for a short cut across
a field. And the moon went with him.

The short cut led right to where Harold thought a forest ought to be.

He didn't want to get lost in the woods.
So he made a very small forest, with just
one tree in it.

It turned out to be an apple tree.

The apples would be very tasty, Harold
thought, when they got red.

So he put a frightening dragon under the tree to guard the apples.

It was a terribly frightening dragon.

It even frightened Harold. He backed away.

His hand holding the purple crayon shook.

Suddenly he realized what was happening.

But by then Harold was over his head in an ocean.

He came up thinking fast.

And in no time he was climbing aboard a
trim little boat.

He quickly set sail.

And the moon sailed along with him.

After he had sailed long enough, Harold made land without much trouble.

He stepped ashore on the beach, wondering
where he was.

The sandy beach reminded Harold of picnics.
And the thought of picnics made him hungry.

So he laid out a nice simple picnic lunch.

There was nothing but pie.

But there were all nine kinds of pie that
Harold liked best.

When Harold finished his picnic there was quite a lot left.

He hated to see so much delicious pie go to waste.

So Harold left a very hungry moose and a
deserving porcupine to finish it up.

And, off he went, looking for a hill to
climb, to see where he was.

Harold knew that the higher up he went,
the farther he could see. So he decided
to make the hill into a mountain.

If he went high enough, he thought, he could see the window of his bedroom.

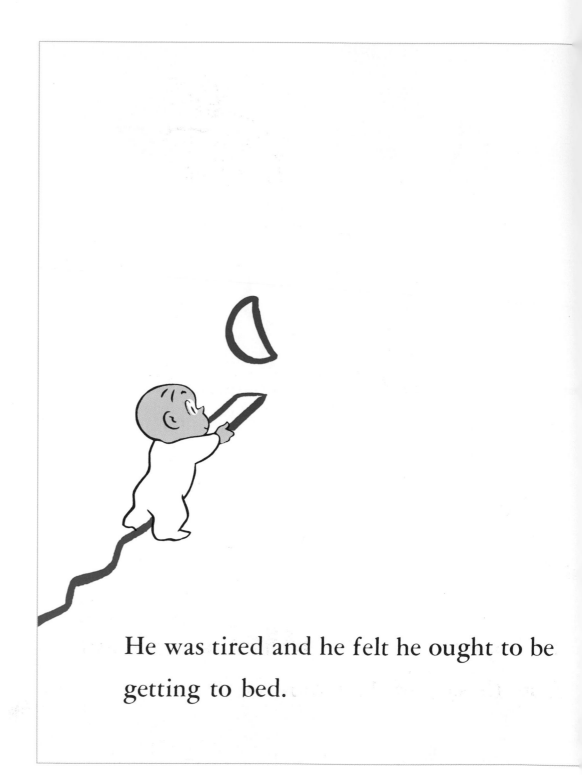

He was tired and he felt he ought to be getting to bed.

He hoped he could see his bedroom window
from the top of the mountain.

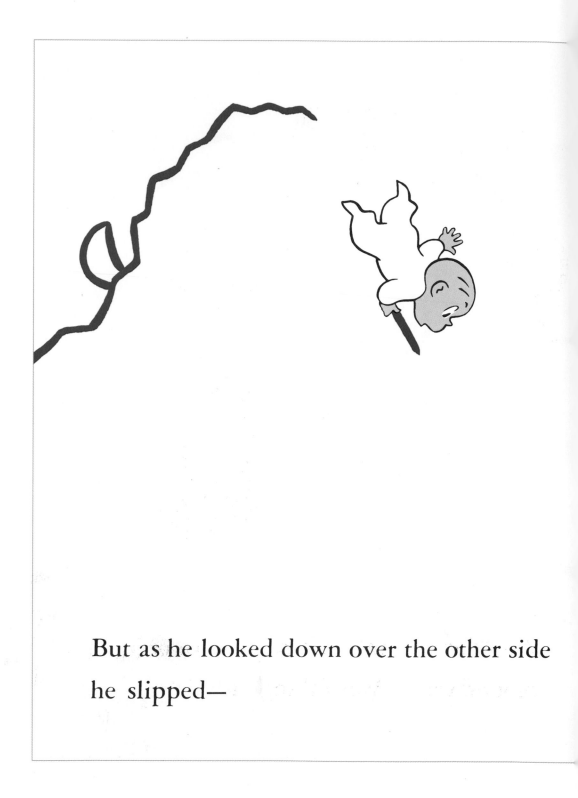

But as he looked down over the other side
he slipped—

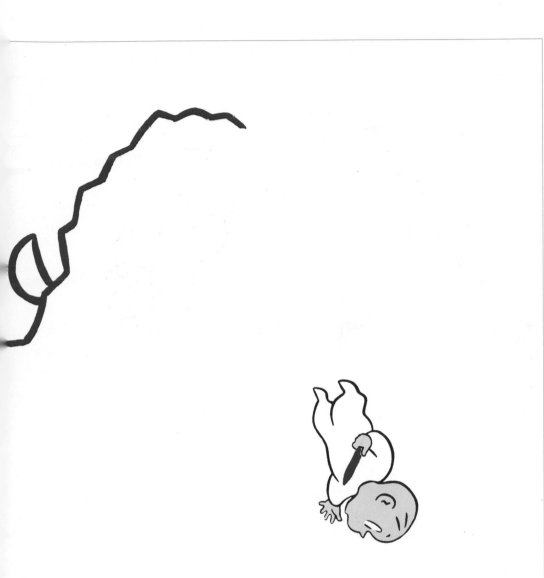

And there wasn't any other side of the mountain. He was falling, in thin air.

But, luckily, he kept his wits and his purple crayon.

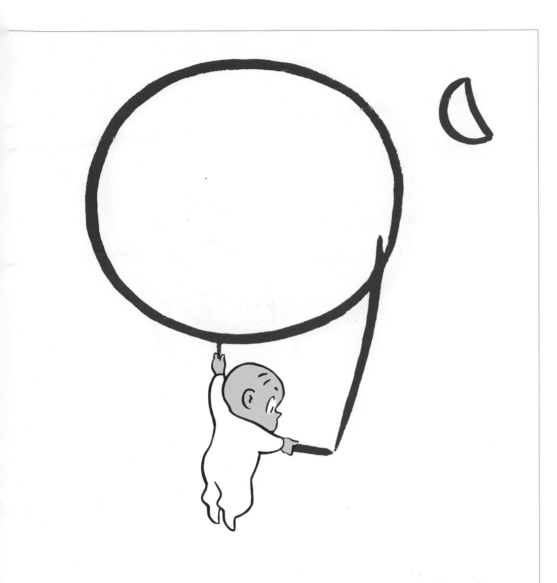

He made a balloon and he grabbed on to it.

And he made a basket under the balloon big enough to stand in.

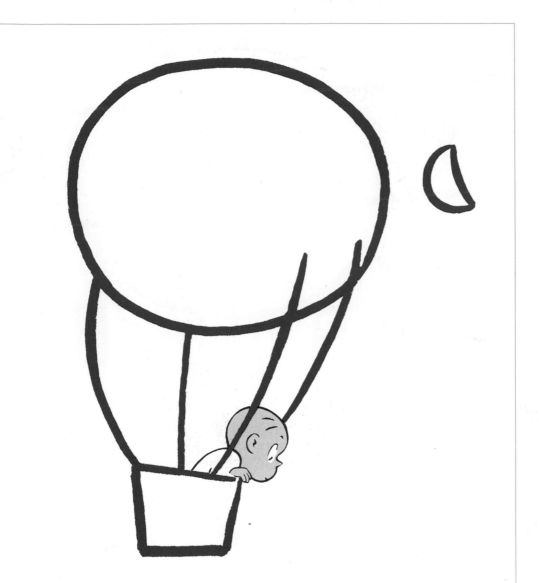

He had a fine view from the balloon but he
couldn't see his window. He couldn't even
see a house.

So he made a house, with windows.

And he landed the balloon on the grass in
the front yard.

None of the windows was his window.

He tried to think where his window ought
to be.

He made some more windows.

He made a big building full of windows.

He made lots of buildings full of windows.

He made a whole city full of windows.

But none of the windows was his window.

He couldn't think where it might be.

He decided to ask a policeman.

The policeman pointed the way Harold was
going anyway. But Harold thanked him.

And he walked along with the moon,
wishing he was in his room and in bed.

Then, suddenly, Harold remembered.

He remembered where his bedroom window was, when there was a moon.

It was always right around the moon.

And then Harold made his bed.

He got in it and he drew up the covers.

The purple crayon dropped on the floor.
And Harold dropped off to sleep.

HAROLD *and the* PURPLE CRAYON

1955

But, luckily, he kept his wits and his purple crayon.

Harold is representative of every child; he is a creator and a person of action. His imagination empowers him but also brings him safely back to his bedroom. He has the magical ability to create two-dimensional worlds that satisfy the needs of his three-dimensional being.

The enduring popularity of Harold and his purple crayon continues to remind readers that a good book doesn't have to be big and splashy, or even have a lot of color in it. Harold lives on in children's imaginations because he lives out the fantasies of all children.

How to enjoy *Harold and the Purple Crayon* further:

- Draw an adventure with your child—start the picture with one line, and have the child continue it with another line.
- Talk with your child about the different emotions that Harold experiences. Was your child worried when the dragon scared Harold? How did your child feel when Harold fell off the mountain?
- Reverse the colors of Harold by using a white crayon on a purple piece of paper.
- Encourage your child to draw his or her own fantasy stories. Where would he or she like to go? What is your child afraid of, and how would he or she conquer those things?
- The moon is an important symbol on every page: a reminder of constancy and security, something a child can point to no matter what is happening to Harold. Help your child find the moon throughout the book.

Crockett Johnson (1906–1975) was the pseudonym used by David Johnson Leisk, a cartoonist and an art director. Johnson drew weekly cartoon panels for *Collier's*, and his syndicated newspaper comic strip, "Barnaby," ran from 1941 to 1962. As an illustrator, he produced over thirty books for children; his simple line, sophisticated composition, and sweet humor are consistent throughout his work. Many other Harold books have remained favorites since their publication in the 1950s, including *Harold's Fairy Tale, Harold's Trip to the Sky, Harold at the North Pole, Harold's Circus, A Picture for Harold's Room,* and *Harold's ABC*. Johnson collaborated with his wife, writer and poet Ruth Krauss, on *The Carrot Seed*, another perennial favorite.

tomi Ungerer

CRICTOR

For Nancy, Ursula and Susan

Once upon a time in a little French town

lived an old lady whose name was Madame Louise Bodot.

She had one son who was in Africa studying reptiles.

One morning the mailman brought her a peculiar O-shaped box

Madame Bodot screamed when she opened it.

It was a snake her son had sent her for her birthday.

To make sure it was not a poisonous snake, she went to the zoo.
She identified it as a boa constrictor. So she called her animal
Crictor.

Madame Bodot mothered her new pet, feeding it bottles of milk.

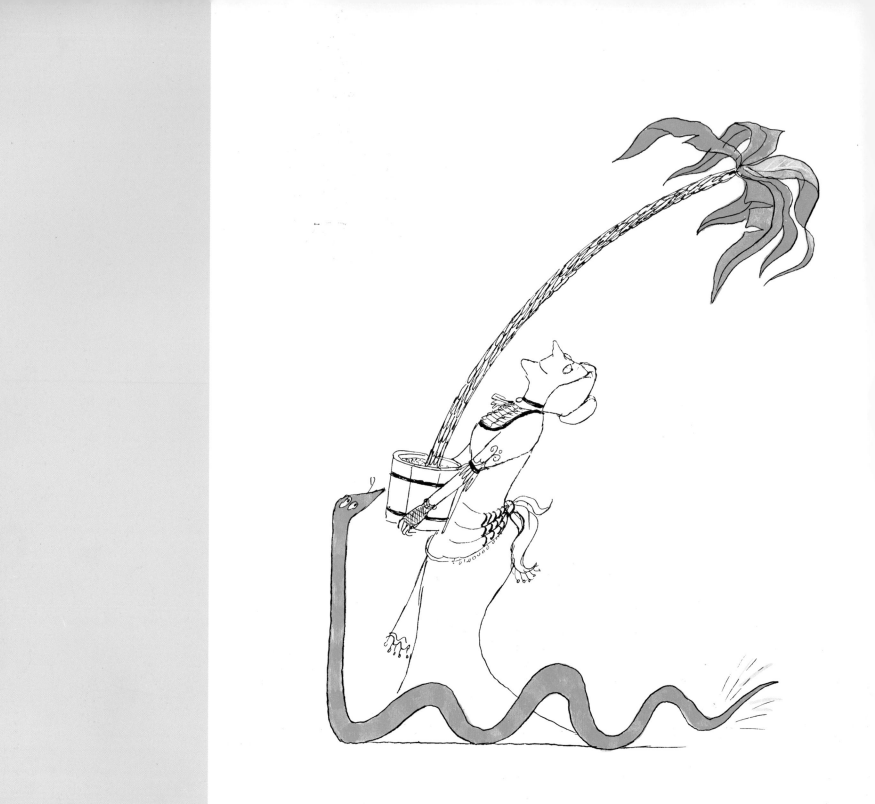

She bought palm trees so Crictor would really feel at home.

As dogs do when they are happy, he wagged his tail.

Well fed, Crictor grew longer and longer and stronger and stronger.

The boa followed his mistress when she went shopping.

Everyone was astonished.

Madame Bodot knitted a long woolen sweater
for her pet to wear on cold days.

Crictor also had a warm, comfortable bed.

There he would dream happily, under his palm trees.

In the winter it was fun for Crictor to wriggle in the snow.

Madame Bodot taught at the public school.

One day she decided to take Crictor to her classes.

Soon Crictor learned to shape the alphabet in his own way.

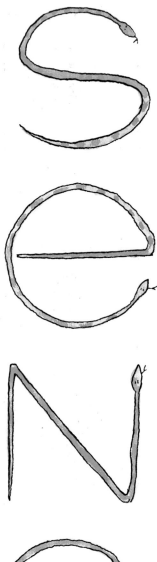

as in snake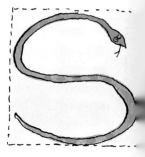

as in elephant

as in nothing

as in Oak

as in lion

as in man

as in glass

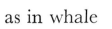

as in whale

He could count too, forming figures.

 for your two hands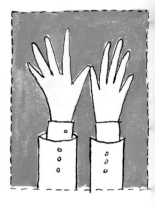

 for the three little pigs

for the four legs of the dog

for your five fingers

for the six legs of a bug

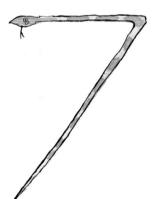

for the seven dwarfs

for the eight arms of the octopus

The boa liked to play with little boys

and little girls too.

He helped the boy scouts learn knots.

Crictor was a helpful snake.

One day in a sidewalk cafe Madame Bodot heard from a friend

at the next table that there had been a series of thefts in the town.

That very night the burglar broke into her apartment.

Madame Bodot was already gagged and tied to a chair
when the faithful boa awoke and furiously attacked the
burglar. The villain's terrified shrieks awoke the neighbors.

Crictor remained coiled around him until the police arrived.

For his bravery a nice medal was awarded to the heroic snake.

Crictor even inspired the local sculptor to make a statue in his honor.

And the city dedicated a park to him.

Loved and respected by the entire village,

Crictor lived a long and happy life.

The End

CRICTOR

1958

Crictor was a helpful snake.

Every child longs for a pet—but what if the pet were as exotic and helpful as this particular boa constrictor? Madame Bodot's clever companion is funny and heroic, as well as being very adaptable, which is not a bad message to send to resistant young children. This playful fantasy also reinforces the positive idea that kindness and good deeds will always be rewarded.

Tomi Ungerer's simple—even snakelike—line is combined with two bright preseparated colors to create one of his most memorable characters.

How to enjoy *Crictor* further:

+ Point out all of the different shapes that Crictor can make.
+ Have your child create his or her own letters, numbers, and shapes from modeling clay or a cooked noodle.
+ Ask your child to identify a hero. What does it take to be a hero?
+ Discuss with your child what kind of unusual pet he or she would choose and why.

Tomi Ungerer was born in 1931 in Strasbourg, France, and grew up during the Great Depression and the turmoil of World War II. He studied at the École des Arts Decoratifs in Strasbourg and also traveled on foot across Europe, where he received the greatest part of his education by hitchhiking, doing odd jobs, and constantly drawing and painting. In 1956 he immigrated to the United States. Harper & Brothers published his first children's book, *The Mellops Go Flying*, in 1957, and, in later years, three more books about the same clever pigs. Revered for his charming, masterful satire, and often macabre humor, Ungerer is the author and illustrator of over forty books for children, including many beloved classics: *Emile*, *Moon Man*, *The Three Robbers*, and *The Beast of Monsieur Racine*.

A BABY SISTER FOR FRANCES

by RUSSELL HOBAN

Pictures by LILLIAN HOBAN

It was a quiet evening.
Father was reading his newspaper.
Mother was feeding Gloria, the new baby.
Frances was sitting under the kitchen sink.
She was singing a little song:

Plinketty, plinketty, plinketty, plink,
Here is the dishrag that's under the sink.
Here are the buckets and brushes and me,
Plinketty, plinketty, plinketty, plee.

She stopped the song and listened.
Nobody said anything.

Frances went to her room and took some gravel
out of the drawer where she had been saving it.
She put the gravel into her empty coffee can
and put the lid back on the can.
Frances marched into the living room
and rattled the gravel in the can.
As she marched she sang a marching song:

Here we go marching, rattley bang!

"Please don't do that, Frances," said Father.
Frances stopped.
"All right," she said.
She went back to the kitchen and sat down under the sink.
Mother came in, carrying Gloria.
"Why are you sitting under the sink?" said Mother.
"I like it here," said Frances. "It's cozy."
"Would you like to help me put Gloria to bed?" said Mother.

"How much allowance does Gloria get?" said Frances.
"She is too little to have an allowance," said Father.
"Only big girls like you get allowances.
Isn't it nice to be a big sister?"
"May I have a penny along with my nickel
now that I am a big sister?" said Frances.
"Yes," said Father. "Now your allowance
will be six cents a week because you are a big sister."
"Thank you," said Frances.
"I know a girl who gets seventeen cents a week.
She gets three nickels and two pennies."
"Well," said Father, "it's time for bed now."
Father picked Frances up from under the sink
and gave her a piggyback ride to bed.

Mother and Father tucked her in and kissed her good night.
"I need my tiny special blanket," said Frances.
Mother gave her the tiny special blanket.
"And I need my tricycle and my sled
and both teddy bears
and my alligator doll," said Frances.
Father brought in the tricycle and the sled
and both teddy bears and the alligator doll.
Mother and Father kissed her good night again
and Frances went to sleep.

In the morning Frances got up and washed
and began to dress for school.
"Is my blue dress ready for me to wear?" said Frances.
"Oh, dear," said Mother, "I was so busy with Gloria
that I did not have time to iron it,
so you'll have to wear the yellow one."
Mother buttoned Frances up the back.
Then she brushed her hair and put a new ribbon in it
and put her breakfast on the table.
"Why did you put sliced bananas on the oatmeal?"
said Frances.
"Did you forget that I like raisins?"
"No, I did not forget," said Mother,
"but you finished up the raisins yesterday
and I have not been out shopping yet."

"Well," said Frances, "things are not very good
around here anymore. No clothes to wear.
No raisins for the oatmeal.
I think maybe I'll run away."
"Finish your breakfast," said Mother.
"It is almost time for the school bus."
"What time will dinner be tonight?" said Frances.
"Half past six," said Mother.
"Then I will have plenty of time to run away
after dinner," said Frances,
and she kissed her mother good-bye
and went to school.

After dinner that evening
Frances packed her little knapsack very carefully.
She put in her tiny special blanket and her alligator doll.
She took all of the nickels and pennies
out of her bank, for travel money,
and she took her good luck coin for good luck.
Then she took a box of prunes from the kitchen
and five chocolate sandwich cookies.

"Well," said Frances, "it is time to say good-bye.
I am on my way. Good-bye."
"Where are you running away to?" said Father.
"I think that under the dining-room table is the best place,"
said Frances. "It's cozy,
and the kitchen is near if I run out of cookies."
"That is a good place to run away to," said Mother,
"but I'll miss you."
"I'll miss you too," said Father.
"Well," said Frances, "good-bye," and she ran away.

Father sat down with his newspaper.

Mother took up the sweater she was knitting.

Father put down the newspaper.

"You know," he said, "it is not the same house without Frances."

"That is just *exactly* what I was thinking," said Mother.

"The place seems lonesome and empty without her."

Frances sat under the dining-room table and ate her prunes.

"Even Gloria," said Mother, "as small as she is,
can feel the difference."

"I can hear her crying a little right now," said Father.

"Well," said Mother, "a girl looks up to an older sister.
You know that."

Father picked up his newspaper.
Then he put it down again.
"I miss the songs that Frances used to sing," he said.
"I was *so* fond of those little songs," said Mother.
"Do you remember the one about the tomato?
'What does the tomato say, early in the dawn?'" sang Mother.
"'Time to be all red again, now that night is gone,'" sang Father.
"Yes," he said, "that is a good one, but my favorite

has always been: 'When the wasps and the bumblebees
have a party, nobody comes that can't buzz. . . .'"
"Well," said Mother, "we shall just have to
get used to a quiet house now."

Frances ate three of the sandwich cookies
and put the other two aside for later.
She began to sing:

I am poor and hungry here, eating prunes and rice.
Living all alone is not really very nice.

She had no rice, but chocolate sandwich cookies
did not sound right for the song.

"I can almost hear her now," said Father,
humming the tune that Frances had just sung.
"She has a charming voice."
"It is just not a *family* without Frances," said Mother.
"Babies are very nice. Goodness knows I *like* babies,
but a baby is not a family."
"Isn't that a fact!" said Father.
"A family is *everybody all together.*"

215

"Remember," said Mother, "how I used to say,
'Think how lucky the new baby will be
to have a sister like Frances'?"
"I remember that very well," said Father,
"and I hope that Gloria turns out
to be as clever and good as Frances."
"With a big sister like Frances to help her along,
she ought to turn out just fine," said Mother.
"I'd like to hear from Frances," said Father,
"just to know how she is getting along in her new place."
"I'd like to hear from Frances too," said Mother,
"and I'm not sure the sleeves are right
on this sweater I'm knitting for her."

"Hello," called Frances from the dining room.
"I am calling on the telephone. Hello, hello,
this is me. Is that you?"

"Hello," said Mother. "This is us. How are you?"
"I am fine," said Frances. "This is a nice place,
but you miss your family when you're away. How are you?"
"We are all well," said Father, "but we miss you too."
"I will be home soon," said Frances, and she hung up.

"She said that she will be home soon," said Father.
"That is good news indeed," said Mother.
"I think I'll bake a cake."
Frances put on her knapsack and sang
a little traveling song:

Big sisters really have to stay
At home, not travel far away,
Because everybody misses them
And wants to hug-and-kisses them.

"I'm not sure about that last rhyme," said Frances
as she arrived in the living room
and took off her knapsack.
"That's a good enough rhyme," said Father.
"I like it fine," said Mother,
and they both hugged and kissed her.

"What kind of cake are you baking?" said Frances to Mother.

"Chocolate," said Mother.

"It's too bad that Gloria's too little to have some,"
said Frances, "but when she's a big girl like me,
she can have chocolate cake too."

"Oh, yes," said Mother, "you may be sure that
there will always be plenty of chocolate cake around here."

The End

A BABY SISTER FOR FRANCES

1964

"Well," said Frances, "things are not very good around here anymore. . . . I think maybe I'll run away."

There is no more monumental shift in a child's life than the arrival of a new sibling. Countless picture books have attempted to help children cope with the grim reality of having to share their parents with another person; *A Baby Sister for Frances* summarizes the problems with humor and affection.

Russell Hoban's wry dialogue is lovingly extended by the artwork of Lillian Hoban. When *A Baby Sister for Frances* was first published, the illustrations were done in black and white with an additional two colors. The artist added full color to the original line and halftone drawings in 1993.

How to enjoy *A Baby Sister for Frances* further:

+ If there is a new baby in your family, help your child identify everything that is different since the baby arrived. Then point out how many things are the same, especially that the child is still loved.
+ What kind of care do new babies demand? Discuss with your child different things to do to help out with the new baby.
+ Every child wants to run away from home at some point. Pretend your child is running away! Help him or her pack and decide where to go. (Under the dining room table is a great place.)
+ Frances's mother says, "A family is *everybody all together*." Discuss the meaning of family with your child.

Russell Hoban (born in 1925) was a commercial illustrator who did magazine covers and other work for publications including *Time* and *Sports Illustrated* before becoming a children's book author. The first in his series of classic Frances books, *Bedtime for Frances*, was published in 1960, with illustrations by Garth Williams. Hoban collaborated with his wife, Lillian Hoban, on all the subsequent Frances books, including *A Baby Sister for Frances*, *Bread and Jam for Frances*, *Best Friends for Frances*, and *A Bargain for Frances*. Hoban's gentle wit and clever observations permeate his picture books. He is also the author of the classic children's novel *The Mouse and His Child*. In addition to over sixty-five books for children, Hoban has also written a number of adult novels, including *Riddley Walker*.

Lillian Hoban (1925–1998) was educated at the Philadelphia Museum School of Art and studied modern dance with pioneer Martha Graham. She danced professionally and later taught dance. She illustrated her first book, *Herman the Loser*, by Russell Hoban, in 1961. She went on to illustrate the Frances series and other books by Hoban, as well as over a hundred books by other authors. She also wrote and illustrated dozens of her own original books, creating such classic characters as Arthur the chimp and his sister Violet, some of the most popular characters in the I Can Read series. Her animal characters, usually rendered in colored pastels, perfectly capture the expressions and emotions of very young children.

Leo the Late Bloomer

BY ROBERT KRAUS • PICTURES BY JOSE ARUEGO

For Ken Dewey

J. A.

For Pamela, Bruce
and Billy

R. K.

Leo couldn't do anything right.

He couldn't read.

He couldn't write.

owl
Elephant
Snake
PLOVER
Crocodile

He couldn't draw.

He was a sloppy eater.

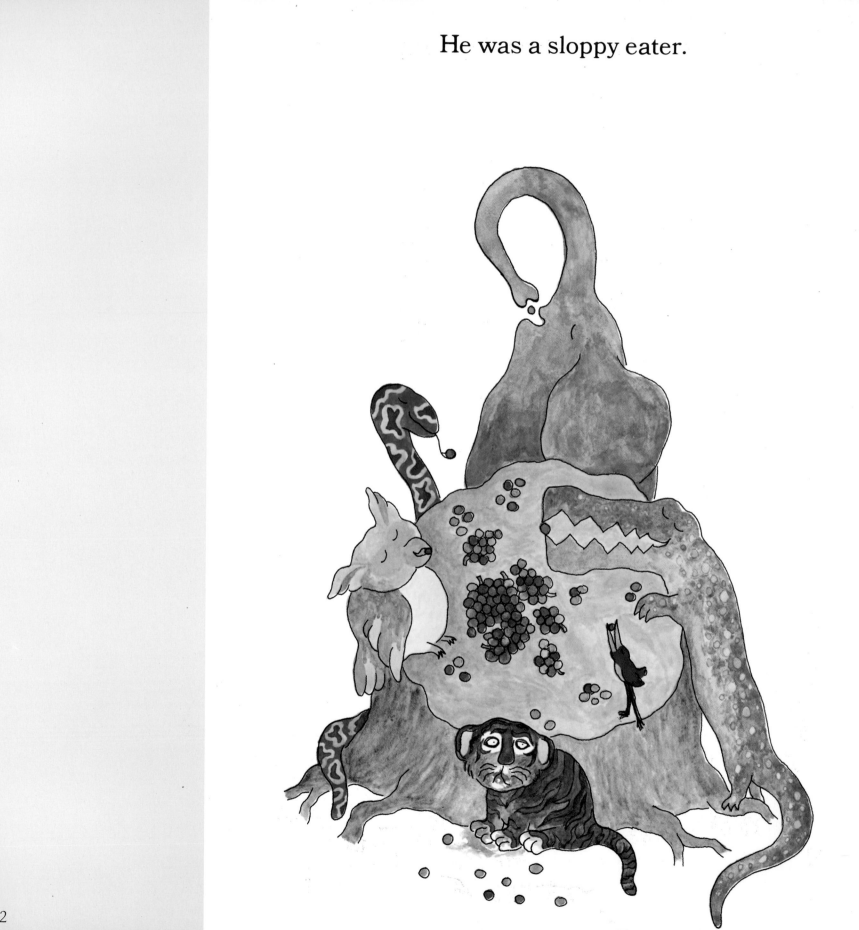

And, he never said a word.

HOOT!

THRUMP!

HISS!

PIP!

CRUNCH!

"What's the matter with Leo?"
asked Leo's father.
"Nothing," said Leo's mother.
"Leo is just a late bloomer."
"Better late than never," thought Leo's father.

Every day Leo's father watched him
for signs of blooming.

And every night Leo's father watched him
for signs of blooming.

"Are you sure Leo's a bloomer?"
asked Leo's father.
"Patience," said Leo's mother.
"A watched bloomer doesn't bloom."

So Leo's father watched television
instead of Leo.

The snows came.
Leo's father wasn't watching.
But Leo still wasn't blooming.

The trees budded.
Leo's father wasn't watching.
But Leo still wasn't blooming.

Then one day,
in his own good time,
Leo bloomed!

He could read!

He could write!

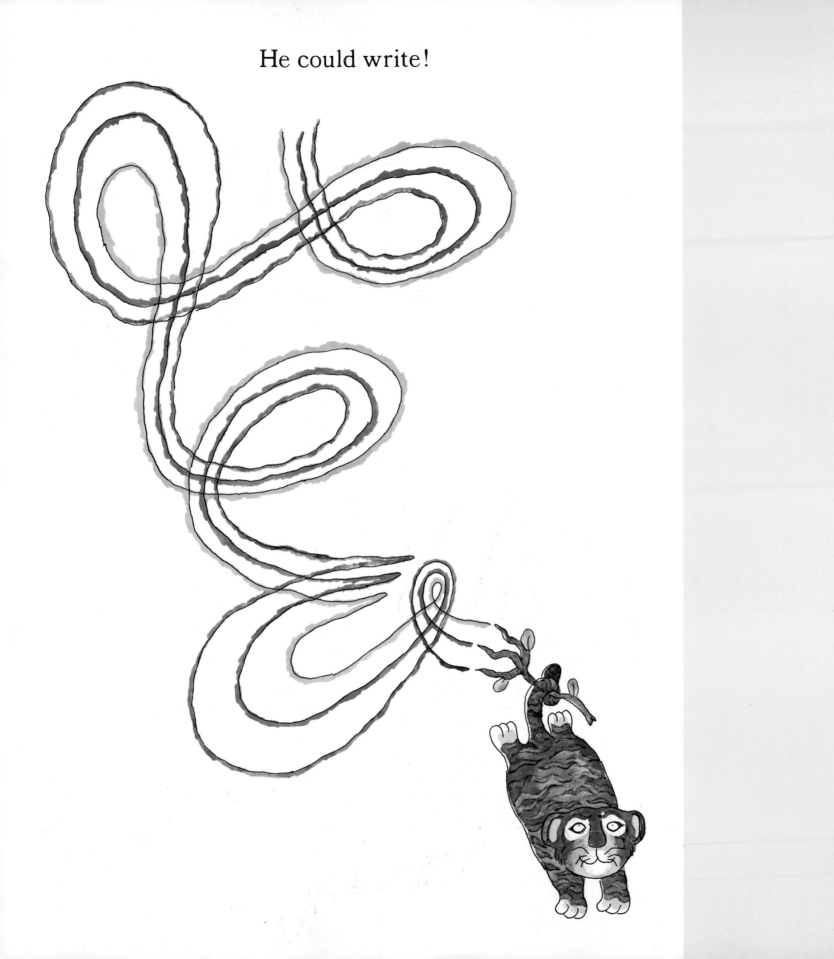

He could draw!

He ate neatly!

He also spoke.
And it wasn't just a word.
It was a whole sentence.
And that sentence was...

"I made it!"

Leo the Late Bloomer

1971

Then one day, in his own good time, Leo bloomed!

The story of *Leo the Late Bloomer* captures one of the prevailing thoughts of the early 1970s: "It's okay to be me." This message is one that parents and children return to again and again, as expectations for children's achievement in school—and in life in general—continue to accelerate. Many closet underachievers need to be told that one day they will bloom, especially if their parents don't pressure them so much about it. *Leo the Late Bloomer* offers empowerment and hope. Leo's resonant first sentence says it all: "I made it!"

How to enjoy *Leo the Late Bloomer* further:

+ Ask your child to name someone who seems sad. Discuss what your child can do to make that person feel better.
+ If your child has difficulty accomplishing some things, or feels frustrated about an inability to do something that other children are doing, talk with your child about being patient. Use Leo as an example to show how everyone grows and develops at his or her own rate.
+ Make a list with your child of the things he or she couldn't accomplish last year, and then make a list of all of the things he or she can now do.
+ Have your child think about something he or she would really like to be able to do. Who would be the best person to ask about it?

Robert Kraus (1925–2001) began his career as a cartoonist, selling his first cartoon when he was ten years old to a newspaper in his hometown, Milwaukee. As a teenager he sold cartoons to national magazines such as *The Saturday Evening Post, Esquire,* and eventually *The New Yorker.* He began writing and illustrating children's books in the 1950s, which led him to start his own publishing company, Windmill Books, in 1965. Windmill quickly established itself as an innovative publisher, with many picture books illustrated by well-known *New Yorker* cartoonists such as Charles Addams and William Steig. Kraus also developed unique formats for children's books, such as the Tubby Books, waterproof bathtub books for very young children. *Leo the Late Bloomer* was originally published by Windmill in 1971; the rights were acquired by HarperCollins in 1977.

Jose Aruego was born in the Philippines. Although most members of his family pursued law as a career, Aruego realized after he completed his law degree in 1955 that he wanted to be an illustrator. He moved to New York City and studied graphic arts and advertising at the Parsons School of Design. In the 1960s he began illustrating books for children, and his recognizable pen-and-ink drawings incorporate his penchant for humor and his love of animals. Many of his most popular books for children are collaborations with Ariane Dewey, including *We Hide, You Seek* and *Look What I Can Do.*

William's Doll

by CHARLOTTE ZOLOTOW

pictures by WILLIAM PÈNE DU BOIS

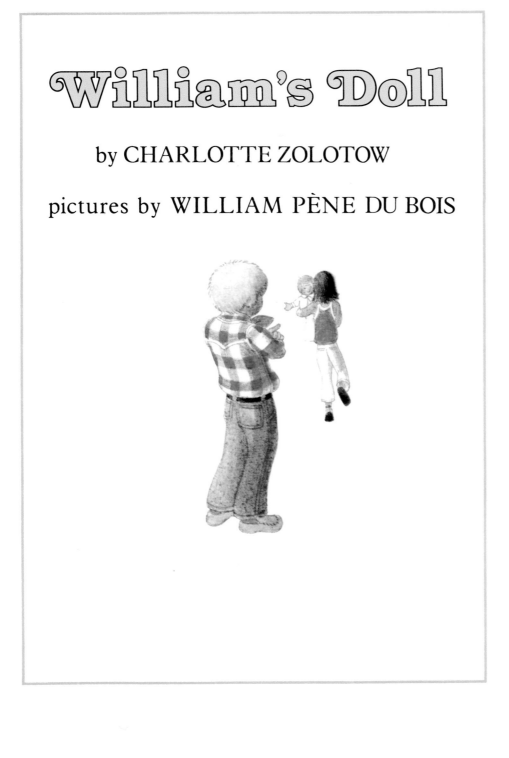

To Billy and Nancy

William wanted a doll.
He wanted to hug it
and cradle it in his arms

and give it a bottle

and take it to the park

and push it in the swing

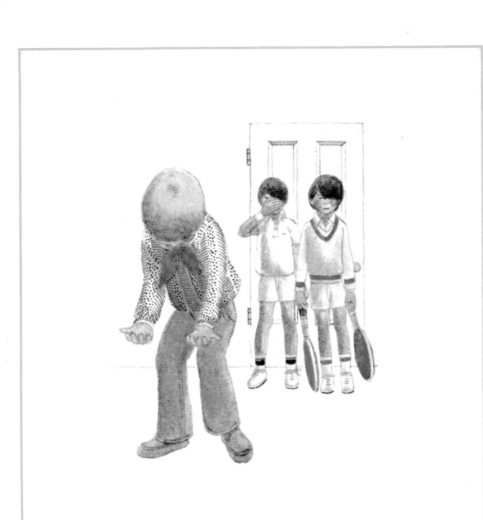

and bring it back home

and undress it

and put it to bed

and pull down the shades
and kiss it goodnight
and watch its eyes close

and then

William wanted to wake it up

in the morning

when the sun came in

and start all over again
just as though he were its father
and it were his child.

"A doll!" said his brother.

"Don't be a creep!"

"Sissy, sissy, sissy!" said the boy next door.

"How would you like a basketball?"
his father said.
But William wanted a doll.
It would have blue eyes
and curly eyelashes
and a long white dress
and a bonnet
and when the eyes closed
they would make a little click
like the doll that belonged
to Nancy next door.
"Creepy" said his brother.
"Sissy sissy" chanted the boy next door.

And his father brought home

a smooth round basketball

and climbed up a ladder

and attached a net to the garage

and showed William

how to jump as he threw the ball

so that it went

through the net

and bounced down

into his arms again.

He practiced a lot

and got good at it
but it had nothing to do

with the doll.
William still wanted one.

His father brought him an electric train.
They set it up on the floor
and made an eight out of the tracks

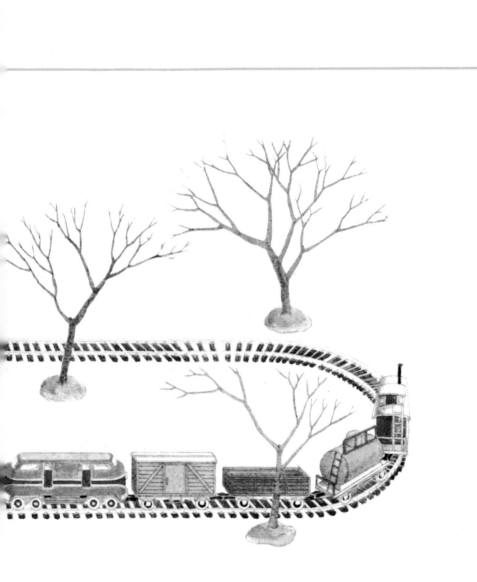

and brought in twigs from outside

and set them in clay

so they looked like trees.

The tiny train
threaded around and around the tracks
with a clacking sound.
William made cardboard stations

and tunnels
and bridges
and played with the train
a lot.

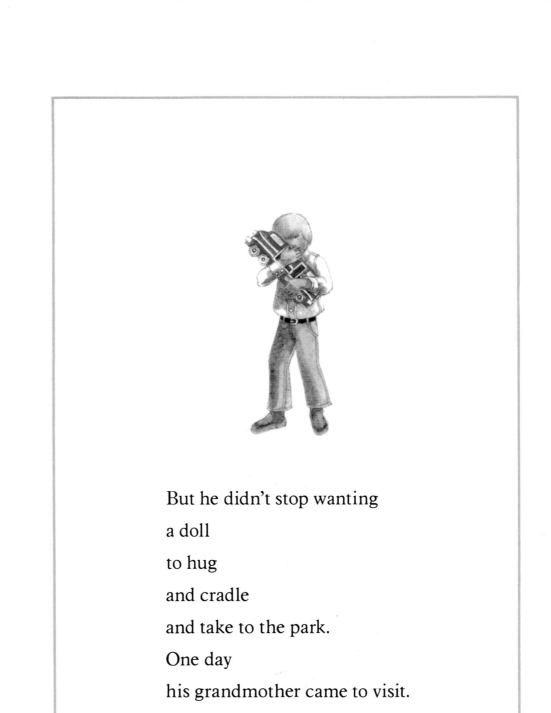

But he didn't stop wanting
a doll
to hug
and cradle
and take to the park.
One day
his grandmother came to visit.

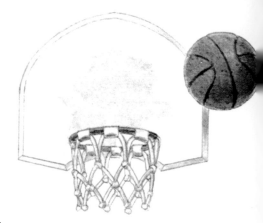

William showed her
how he could throw the ball
through the net
attached to the garage outside.
He showed her the electric train
clacking along the tracks
through the tunnel
over the bridge
around the curve
until it came to a stop
in front of the station
William had made.

She was very interested

and they went for a walk together

and William said,

"but you know

what I really want

is a doll."

"Wonderful," said his grandmother.

"No," William said.

"My brother says

it will make me a creep

and the boy next door

says I'm a sissy

and my father

brings me

other things

instead."

"Nonsense," said his grandmother.

She went to the store and
chose a baby doll
with curly eyelashes
and a long white dress
and a bonnet.
The doll had blue eyes
and when they closed
they made a clicking sound
and William loved it
right away.

But his father was upset.
"He's a boy!" he said
to William's grandmother.
"He has a basketball
and an electric train
and a workbench
to build things with.
Why does he need a doll?"
William's grandmother smiled.
"He needs it," she said,
"to hug
and to cradle
and to take to the park
so that
when he's a father
like you,

he'll know how to
take care of his baby
and feed him
and love him
and bring him
the things he wants,
like a doll
so that he can
practice being
a father."

William's Doll

1972

William wanted a doll.

Is it strange for a little boy to want a doll? In the early 1970s, as people rethought sexual stereotypes, the thought of a boy playing with dolls was revolutionary. (Many people were introduced to *William's Doll* through Marlo Thomas's album *Free to Be You and Me,* one of the liberating forces of the 1970s.) The idea of a boy playing with a doll still makes some people uncomfortable today, but *William's Doll* responds to all of those qualms. Thirty years after publication, the message and story of *William's Doll* are still clear, affirming, and true to the yearnings in a child's heart.

How to enjoy *William's Doll* further:

* Pretend you are taking care of a baby with your child: Cradle it, take it to the park, give it a bottle, and put it to bed.
* Ask your child to think about the different things that we take care of in our lives, and draw a picture of the things that he or she loves.
* Discuss your child's ideas about what are "boy things" and "girl things." The discussion should be nonjudgmental and open-ended.
* Talk with your child about what to do when other children make fun of him or her. Affirm that it's okay to be different.

Charlotte Zolotow was born in Norfolk, Virginia, in 1915. Following her education at the University of Wisconsin, she moved to New York City and began working at Harper's Department of Books for Boys and Girls as a secretary to Ursula Nordstrom. During her long career at Harper & Row—where she was an editor until 1976, then vice president and associate publisher of the Junior Books division, and in 1981, an editorial director of her own imprint, Charlotte Zolotow Books—she also wrote over seventy books for children. Her picture books are noted for their gentle humor, tenderness, and emotional realism. Her many books include *Mr. Rabbit and the Lovely Present,* illustrated by Maurice Sendak (named both a Newbery Honor and Caldecott Honor book); *My Grandson Lew,* illustrated by William Pène du Bois; *I Know a Lady,* illustrated by James Stevenson; and *The Seashore Book,* illustrated by Wendell Minor.

William Pène du Bois (1916–1993) was born in Nutley, New Jersey, and at the age of nineteen published his first children's book. Pène du Bois was born to a family that had long been associated with the arts—painting, stage design, and architecture. He often developed his children's books by creating the illustrations first and then writing the texts, as he believed that children love to look at the pictures first and foremost. Many of his books contain adventure and creative mechanical inventions. Pène du Bois is perhaps best known for his novel *The Twenty-one Balloons,* winner of the Newbery Medal in 1948. During his career Pène du Bois illustrated over fifty books; two were named Caldecott Honor books.

If You Give a Mouse a Cookie

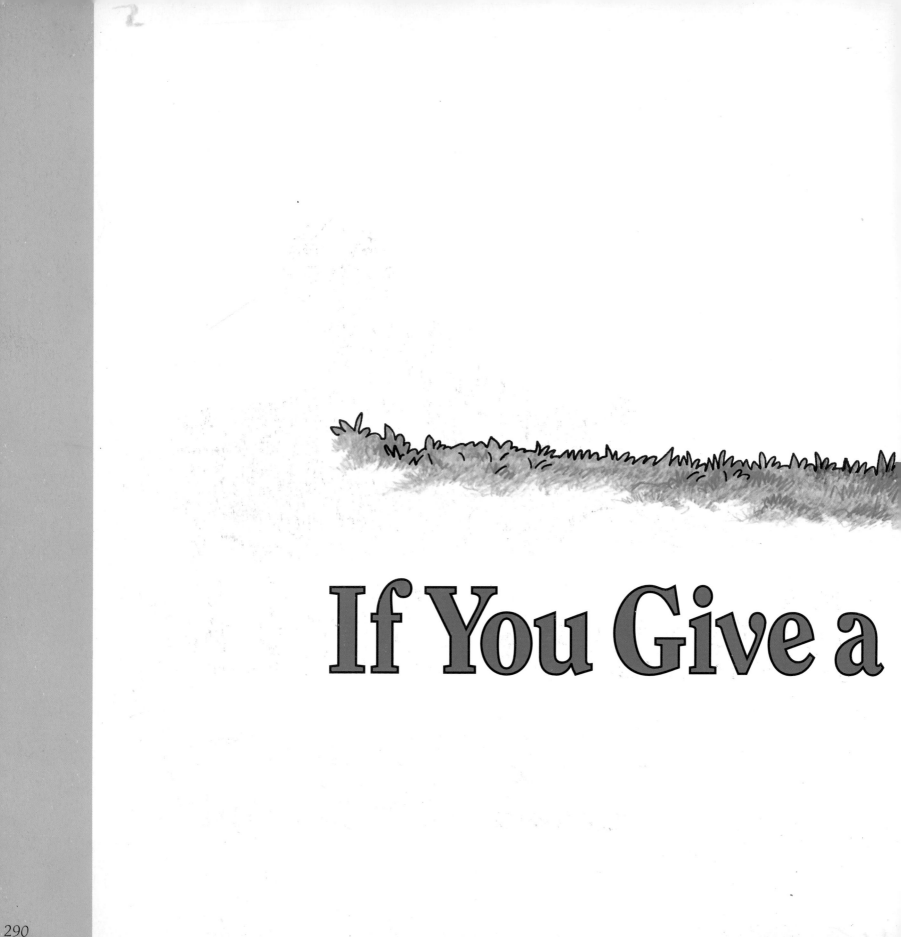

If You Give a

Mouse a Cookie

Laura Joffe Numeroff
ILLUSTRATED BY Felicia Bond

For Florence & William Numeroff,
the two best parents anyone could
ever possibly want! L. J. N.

For Stephen   F. B.

If you give a mouse a cookie,

he's going to ask for a glass of milk.

When you give him the milk,

he'll probably ask you for a straw.

When he's finished, he'll ask for a napkin.

Then he'll want to look in a mirror
to make sure he doesn't
have a milk mustache.

When he looks into the mirror,

he might notice his hair needs a trim.

So he'll probably ask
for a pair of nail scissors.

When he's finished giving himself a trim,
he'll want a broom to sweep up.

He'll start sweeping.

He might get carried away and
sweep every room in the house.

He may even end up washing the floors as well!

When he's done,
he'll probably want to take a nap.

You'll have to fix up a little box for him
with a blanket and a pillow.

He'll crawl in,
make himself comfortable
and fluff the pillow a few times.

He'll probably ask you to read him a story.

So you'll read to him from one of your books,
and he'll ask to see the pictures.

When he looks at the pictures,
he'll get so excited he'll want to draw
one of his own. He'll ask for paper and crayons.

He'll draw a picture.

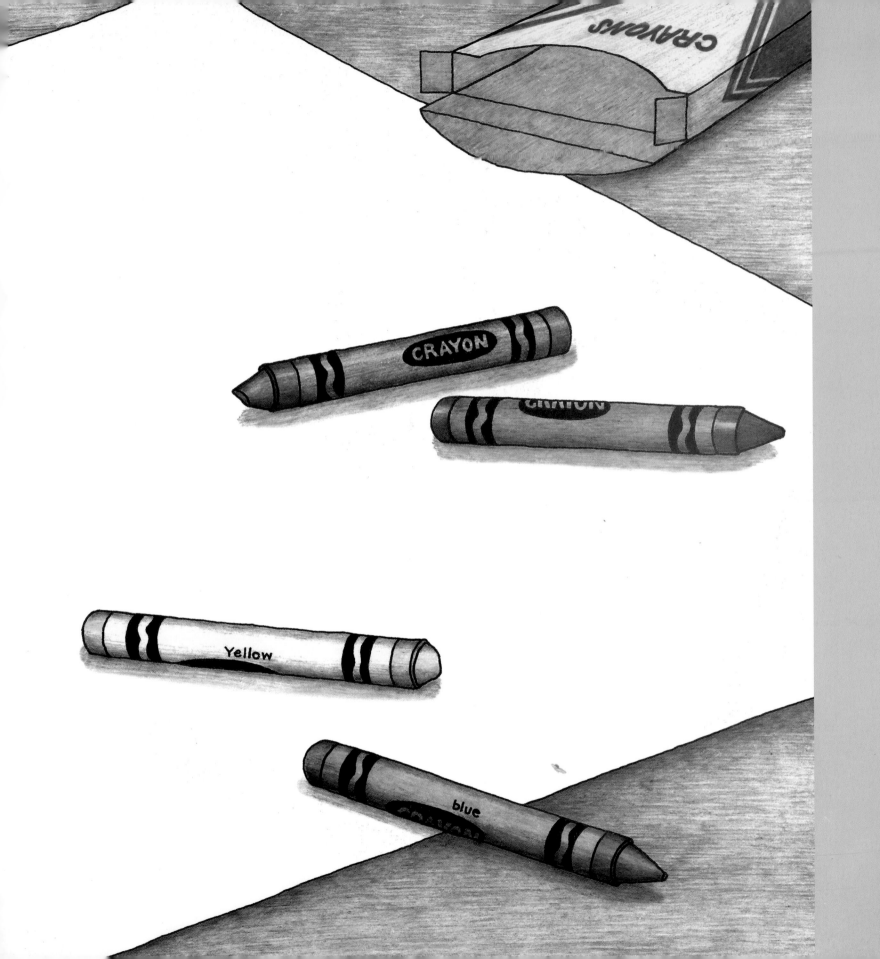

When the picture is finished,

he'll want to sign his name

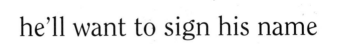

with a pen.

Then he'll want to hang his picture on your refrigerator.

Which means he'll need

313

Scotch tape.

He'll hang up his drawing
and stand back to look at it.

CRACKERS

Looking at the refrigerator
will remind him that

he's thirsty.

So . . .

he'll ask for a glass of milk.

And chances are if he asks for
a glass of milk,

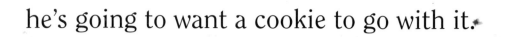
he's going to want a cookie to go with it.

If You Give a Mouse a Cookie

1985

If you give a mouse a cookie, he's going to ask for a glass of milk.

If You Give a Mouse a Cookie has become a cultural phenomenon. One of the reasons may be the satisfying use of words and patterns that are repeated often enough that children can begin to anticipate them. In this book the cause-and-effect pattern dominoes until the story comes full circle, ending the book with its beginning, a cookie. The artwork extends the story with many creative and inventive details and depicts an exuberant little mouse whose moods and immediate desires reflect those of a young child exactly right.

How to enjoy *If You Give a Mouse a Cookie* further:

+ Take advantage of the structure of the story. After reading the first few pages, pause to allow your child to guess what is coming next. By the second reading he or she will be calling out the words before each turn of the page.
+ Have your child make up a story based on a chain reaction. Start the story off by saying: "If you give a _____ a _____ . . ."
+ The mouse draws a picture of his family; have your child draw a picture of his or her family.
+ Make cookies for your mouse!

Laura Joffe Numeroff was born in 1953 in Brooklyn, New York, and was educated at Pratt Institute. Her father was an artist and her mother a teacher; she grew up reading voraciously and drawing pictures. In a class about writing and illustrating children's books, her homework assignment became her first children's book, *Amy for Short,* published in 1976. Numeroff has since published over twenty celebrated books for children. Her classic *If You Give a Mouse a Cookie* was published in 1985; its sequels, including *If You Give a Moose a Muffin, If You Give a Pig a Pancake,* and *If You Take a Mouse to the Movies,* have the same engaging humor and clever chain reactions.

Felicia Bond was born in 1954 to American parents in Yokohama, Japan. After studying at the University of Texas at Austin and working as a botanical illustrator, she moved to New York and became a design assistant at a publishing house, and then an art director of a children's book imprint. In 1983 she began devoting herself full-time to children's book writing and illustration. Her work is characterized by an imaginative richness that has transformed many simple texts into glowing picture books. Bond began working in children's books when illustrations were commonly prepared using color preseparated by the artist; her technical brilliance in the use of this technique is unmatched in the field of illustration.

rge shrinks

by WILLIAM JOYCE

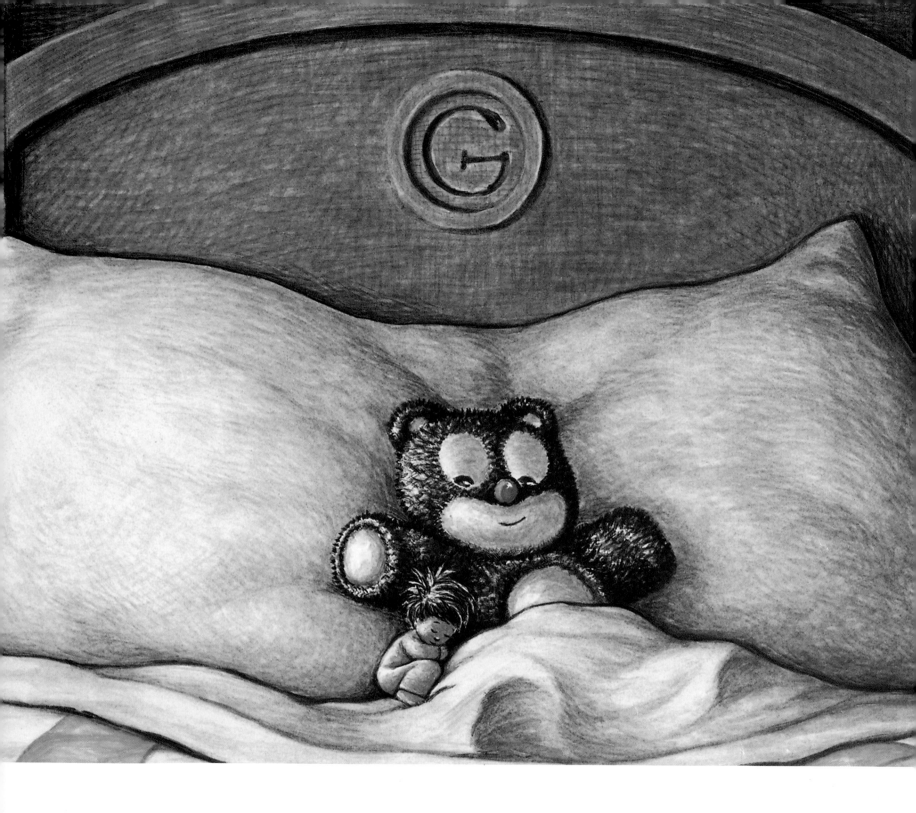

One day, while his mother and father were out, George dreamt he was small, and when he woke up he found it was true.

His parents had left him a note. It read:

"Dear George, when you wake up,

please make your bed,

brush your teeth,

and take a bath.

Then clean up your room

and go get your little brother.

Eat a good breakfast,

and don't forget to wash the dishes, dear.

Do your homework.

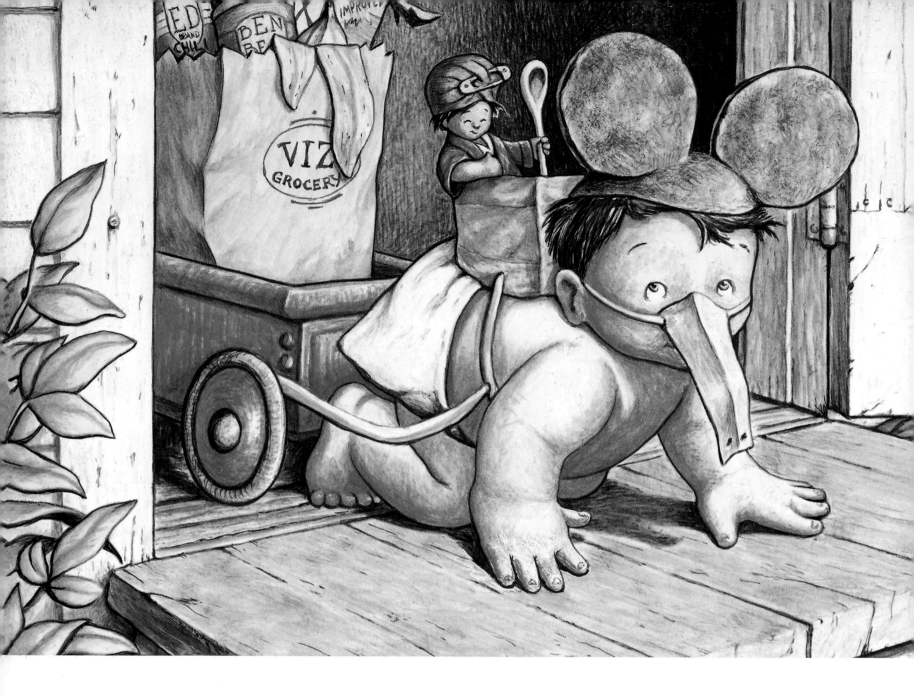

Take out the garbage,

and play quietly.

Make sure you water the plants

and feed the fish.

Then check the mail

and get some fresh air.

344

Try to stay out of trouble,

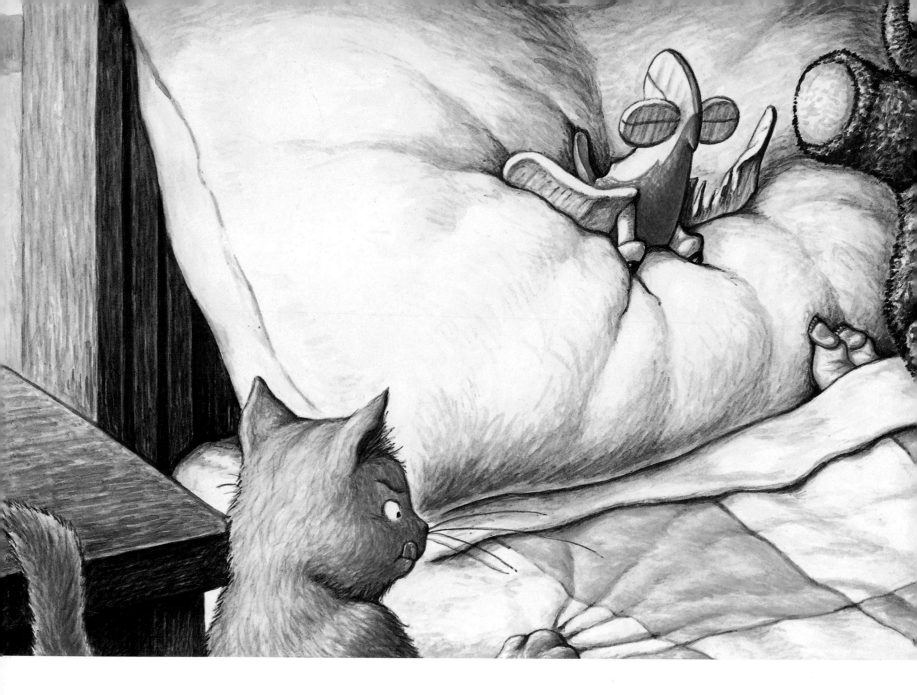

and we'll be home soon.

Love, Mom and Dad."

george shrinks

1985

*One day, while his mother and father were out, George dreamt he was small,
and when he woke up he found it was true.*

Children like the idea of shrinking and growing. After all, they are the small ones living in a grown-up world. *George Shrinks* plays out the common fantasy of becoming tiny, as so many children's stories over the centuries have also done.

George's story is told in a deadpan manner through a letter, and the artwork consistently provides an ironic counterpoint to the words. Even very young children understand the play between words and pictures, and enjoy the humor of George's delightful plight in a world where problems become adventures.

How to enjoy *George Shrinks* further:

♦ Imagine with your child that you are a tiny person living in a giant world. How would you take out the garbage? How would you brush your teeth?

♦ Have your child draw a picture of something in the house that would be scary if he or she were George's size. Then have your child draw a picture of something in the house that would be delightful if he or she were very small.

♦ Ask your child to dictate a note to you, including what the *parents* should do while the child is away all day!

William Joyce was born in 1957 and grew up telling funny stories and creating wacky drawings. He studied illustration and filmmaking at Southern Methodist University, and by the time he graduated from college he had several illustration contracts with New York publishers. In 1985 HarperCollins published *George Shrinks*, the first book he both wrote and illustrated. HarperCollins has since published all of Joyce's major works, including *Dinosaur Bob and His Adventures with the Family Lazardo, A Day with Wilbur Robinson, Bently & egg, Santa Calls, The Leaf Men and the Brave Good Bugs, Buddy, The World of William Joyce Scrapbook,* and the Rolie Polie Olie books. Joyce's illustrations capture an inventive world where anything can happen; his stylish 1930s look manages to be both original and classically retro.

Baby Says

John Steptoe

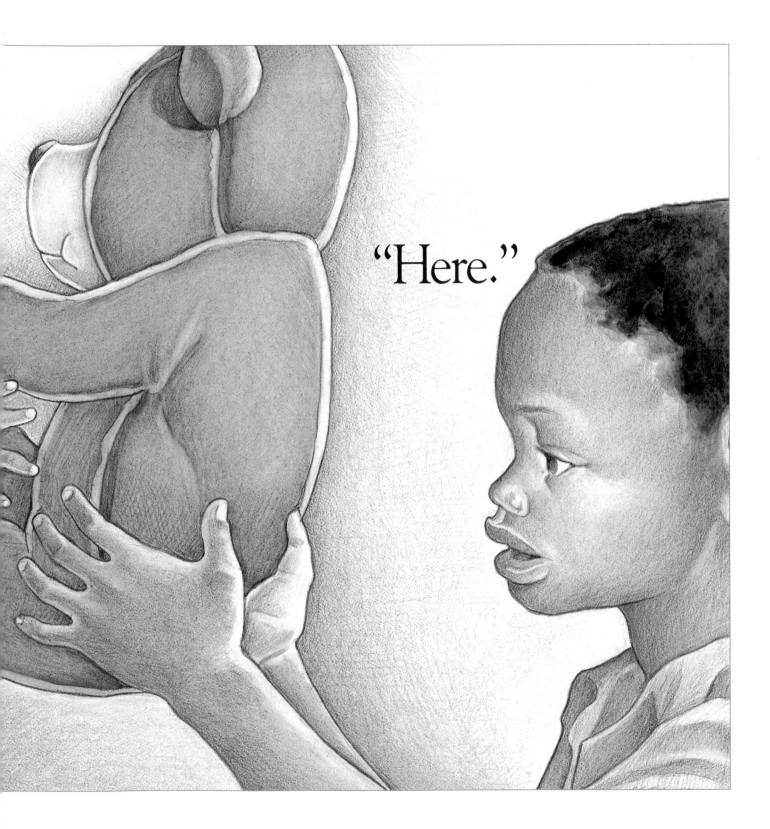

"Here."

"Uh, oh."

"No, no."

"No, no!"

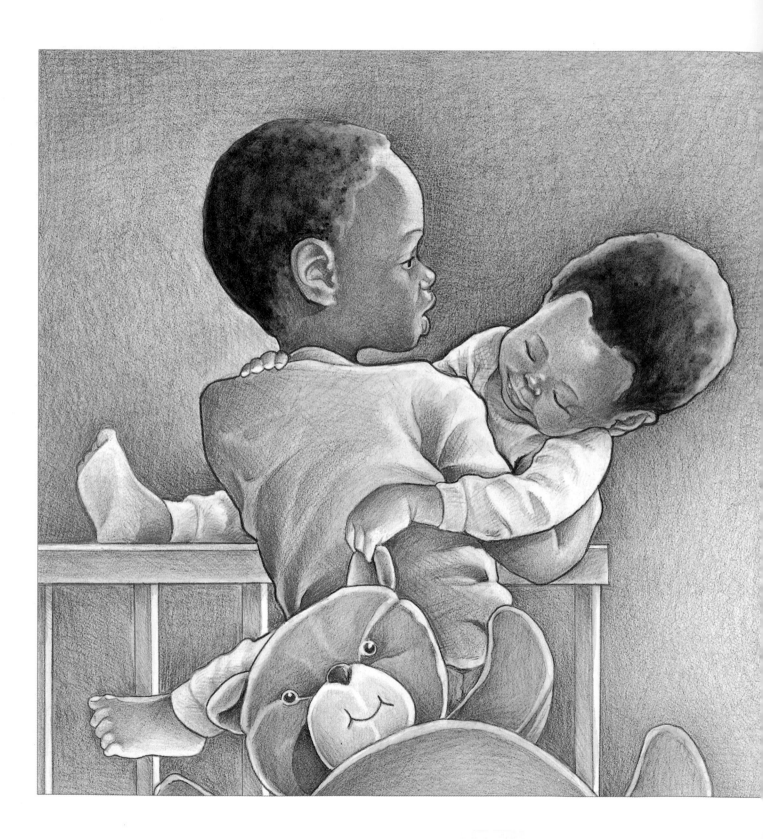

"Okay, okay."

371

"Uh, oh.
No, no."

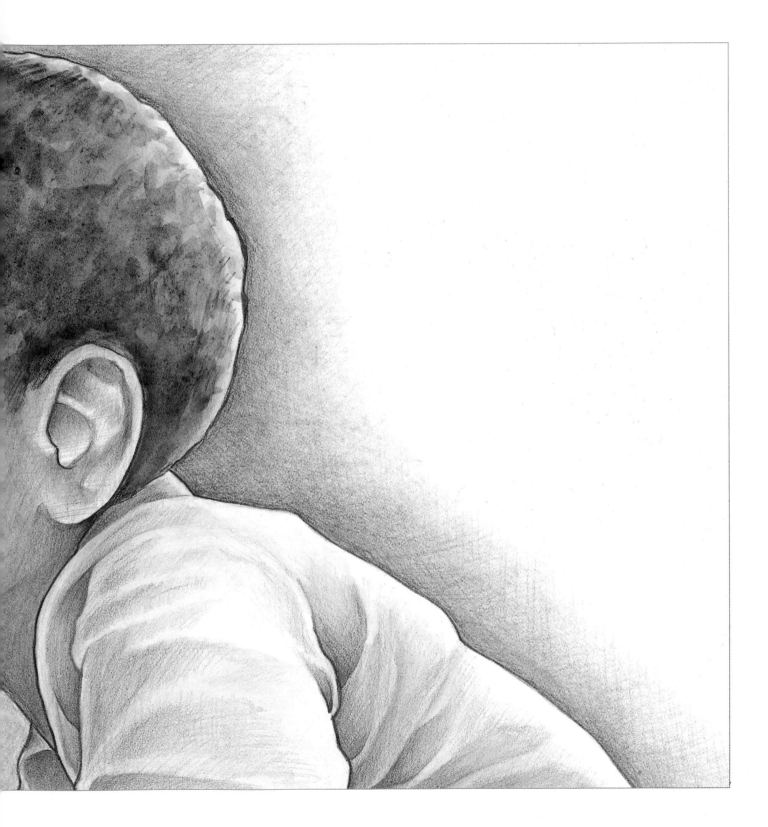

375

"Okay, baby. Okay."

Baby says, "Okay!"

Baby Says

1988

"Uh, oh."

Can a story be told with just seven words? John Steptoe took on that challenge in *Baby Says,* using *uh, oh, here, no, okay, baby,* and *says* to tell a story about two brothers and their sibling rivalry. An amazing range of emotion is communicated through these simple words, extended by the beautifully rendered artwork. Reading this text aloud necessitates a varied inflection of the words; there are of course many ways to read *no* or *uh, oh* depending on the events in the story.

How to enjoy *Baby Says* further:

+ Very young children, even babies and toddlers, will begin to identify the seven words in this book. Read it aloud to them using different tones of voice and hear them repeat it back.
+ Older children, just beginning to read, will also enjoy this book as they learn to recognize the simple words on the page.
+ If there is a baby in your house, ask your child to describe how the baby communicates.
+ If you don't have a baby in the house, ask your child to remember the kinds of games that he or she liked playing when very little.
+ Discuss with your child what's "okay"—what is okay for a baby to do, and what is okay for an older child.

John Steptoe (1950–1989) was born in Brooklyn, New York, and attended the New York School of Art and Design. Before the 1960s, children who were not white were rarely seen in children's picture books. Steptoe was one of the African American talents who helped change the face of publishing. When he was sixteen, he wrote the groundbreaking *Stevie,* which incorporated black characters, black dialogue, and a ghetto setting. Harper & Row published *Stevie* in 1969 with Steptoe's glowing illustrations and, in subsequent years, published *Uptown* and *Train Ride.* Steptoe's work as an author and artist continued to evolve, and he was awarded the Caldecott Honor for both *Mufaro's Beautiful Daughters: An African Tale* and *The Story of Jumping Mouse: A Native American Legend.*

Eric Carle
From Head
to Toe

I am a penguin
and I turn my head.
Can you do it?

I can do it!

I am a giraffe
and I bend my neck.
Can you do it?

I can do it!

I am a buffalo
and I raise my shoulders.
Can you do it?

I can do it!

I am a monkey
and I wave my arms.
                Can you do it?

I am a seal
and I clap my hands.
         Can you do it?

390

I am a gorilla
and I thump my chest.
Can you do it?

I can do it!

I am a cat
and I arch my back.
Can you do it?

I can do it!

I am a crocodile
and I wriggle my hips.
Can you do it?

397

I am a camel
and I bend my knees.
Can you do it?

I can do it!

I am a donkey
and I kick my legs.
Can you do it?

I can do it!

I am an elephant
and I stomp my foot.
Can you do it?

I can do it!

403

I am I
and I wiggle my toe.
Can you do it?

I can do it! I can do it!

From Head to Toe

1997

I can do it!

From Head to Toe invites young children to mimic the simple movements of familiar animals and, in the process, learn to exercise and identify the different parts of the body. The movements suggested in this book have been chosen carefully to encourage participation with the positive, confidence-building message: *I can do it!* As in all of Eric Carle's books, the colorful collages, strikingly designed pages, and rhythmic text create a stimulating interactive experience for children and parents alike.

How to enjoy *From Head to Toe* further:

+ Pick a favorite animal and imitate its movements with your child.
+ Identify various body parts using the pictures in *From Head to Toe*; then have your child draw a self-portrait and identify different body parts.
+ Sing a song such as "Head, Shoulders, Knees, and Toes" with your child.
+ Ask your child which animal he or she would like to be and why.
+ Make a picture using collage art.

Eric Carle was born in 1929 in Syracuse, New York, but grew up in wartime Germany, where he studied graphic arts. He worked as a designer and art director in New York before becoming a children's book author and illustrator. Eric Carle's painted tissue paper collage style is beautifully showcased in more than seventy books for children. He is also widely acclaimed for his innovation in picture-book design. His books incorporate die-cut pages that highlight the themes of the story, whether it be a ladybug who meets bigger and bigger animals as each page is turned in *The Grouchy Ladybug* or a boy who follows clues through the pages of *The Secret Birthday Message*. His texts use repetition, rhythm, alliteration, and concepts that are expertly crafted to entertain his vast preschool audience.

PETE'S A PIZZA

WILLIAM STEIG

PETE'S IN A BAD MOOD. JUST WHEN HE'S SUPPOSED
TO PLAY BALL WITH THE GUYS, IT DECIDES TO RAIN.

PETE'S FATHER CAN'T HELP NOTICING

HOW MISERABLE HIS SON IS.

HE THINKS IT MIGHT CHEER PETE UP

TO BE MADE INTO A PIZZA.

SO HE SETS HIM DOWN ON THE KITCHEN TABLE

AND STARTS KNEADING THE DOUGH

AND STRETCHING IT

THIS WAY AND THAT.

NOW THE DOUGH GETS WHIRLED

AND TWIRLED UP IN THE AIR.

NEXT, SOME OIL IS GENEROUSLY APPLIED.

(IT'S REALLY WATER.)

THEN COMES SOME FLOUR.

(IT'S REALLY TALCUM POWDER.)

AND THEN SOME TOMATOES.

(THEY'RE REALLY CHECKERS.)

PETE CAN'T HELP GIGGLING WHEN HIS MOTHER SAYS

SHE DOESN'T LIKE TOMATOES ON HER PIZZA.

"ALL RIGHT," SAYS HIS FATHER, "NO TOMATOES, JUST SOME CHEESE." (THE CHEESE IS PIECES OF PAPER.)

"HOW ABOUT SOME PEPPERONI, PETEY?"

PETE CAN'T ANSWER BECAUSE HE'S ONLY

SOME DOUGH AND STUFF.

BUT WHEN THAT DOUGH GETS TICKLED,

IT LAUGHS LIKE CRAZY.

"PIZZAS ARE NOT SUPPOSED TO LAUGH!"

"PIZZA-MAKERS ARE NOT SUPPOSED

TO TICKLE THEIR PIZZAS!"

"WELL," SAYS HIS FATHER, "IT'S TIME FOR
THIS PIZZA TO BE PUT IN THE OVEN."

"AH! NOW OUR PIZZA IS NICE AND HOT!"

PETE'S FATHER BRINGS THE PIZZA TO THE TABLE.

"IT'S TIME TO SLICE OUR PIZZA," HE SAYS.

BUT THE PIZZA RUNS AWAY AND

THE PIZZA-MAKER CHASES HIM.

THE PIZZA GETS CAPTURED AND HUGGED.

NOW THE SUN HAS COME OUT.

AND SO THE PIZZA DECIDES TO GO
LOOK FOR HIS FRIENDS.

PETE'S A PIZZA

1998

"Pizzas are not supposed to laugh!"

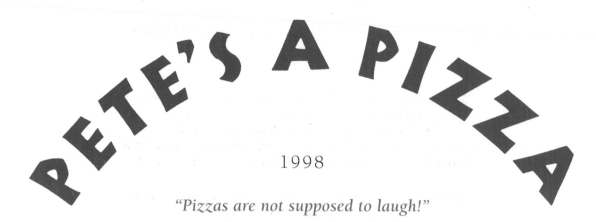

If laughter is the best medicine, it is certainly a good cure for a bad mood. And a dose of love isn't a bad thing either. *Pete's a Pizza* gives parents and grandparents permission to be playful with their children, to love them, and to hug them. Steig's economy of line and his cheerful patterns elevate the comic, cartoon style to an art form.

How to enjoy *Pete's a Pizza* further:

◆ Pretend your child is a pizza! Or re-create any kind of food through dramatic play—bake a pie, make a casserole, or chop a salad. Ask your child what kind of food he or she would most like to be.

◆ Create your own reader's theater—read the story out loud while your child and another adult act it out.

◆ Make a list of other things you could do with your child on a rainy day.

William Steig was born in 1907 in Brooklyn, New York, and studied at City College and the National Academy of Design. He is widely regarded as one of the twentieth century's most significant cartoonists, having created piercingly perceptive drawings for *The New Yorker* since 1930. As a children's book creator, Steig has produced numerous award-winning books, including *Sylvester and the Magic Pebble,* winner of the 1970 Caldecott Medal; *Amos & Boris,* winner of the 1973 National Book Award; *Farmer Palmer's Wagon Ride,* a 1977 Newbery Honor Book; *The Amazing Bone,* a 1977 Caldecott Honor Book; and *Doctor De Soto,* a 1983 Newbery Honor Book. His affectionate humor, rich stories, and signature-style drawings characterize all of his works.

Copyrights and Dedications

Acknowledgments and a Little History

So many talents have contributed to the *HarperCollins Treasury of Picture Book Classics: A Child's First Collection* that it is almost impossible to acknowledge all of them. The picture book is truly a collaborative effort that marries the artistic efforts of a writer and an illustrator with the creative energy, business acumen, and craftsmanship of many zealous individuals in the publishing world.

The form of the picture book for the very young owes much to the work of Lucy Sprague Mitchell, who in the 1920s, along with many prominent child psychologists, developed theories about development in children under the age of five. The idea that the preschool child experiences the world differently than adults do was revolutionary at the time. The obvious correlate to this shift in thought was that stories for preschool children should reflect their experience of the world—literature should be based on a child's concrete interactions and realities as well as his or her own inner life. The old model, based on fairy tales and fables that evolved from an adult's experience of the world, had little to do with a young child's emotional and intellectual development. It was Mitchell who suggested to publisher William R. Scott that Margaret Wise Brown, one of her students, would be the right editor to head up his new line of young children's picture books. Scott's list, launched in 1938, became known for its sensitivity in addressing topics just right for the very young child.

The work of Mitchell, Brown, and Scott, as well as the work of librarians and of other prominent publishers of the time, laid the foundation for the very young picture book. All of the books in this collection share some universal qualities: They tap into children's emotions; the stories are told with language that endures repeated readings because of its poetry and simplicity; the artwork extends the text so that the whole of the book is always more than the sum of its parts. And each of the books in this collection represents the work of a major contributor to the field of children's literature, and also captures something significant about the time in which it was published.

One of the primary reasons HarperCollins has published so many picture book treasures is the existence of one important person: Ursula Nordstrom. Harper & Brothers had created a children's book division in 1926, but it was not until the spectacularly witty, intelligent, charming (and sometimes difficult) Ursula Nordstrom became the editor of Junior Books in 1941 that the department came into its own. Nordstrom was always on the lookout for talent, and many of the greatest authors and illustrators of the twentieth century were published under her shrewd and devoted care: Margaret Wise Brown, Clement Hurd, Crockett Johnson, Maurice Sendak, John Steptoe, Lillian and Russell Hoban, and Charlotte Zolotow—to name just a few.

Nordstrom believed that picture books should not have an obvious message, but should capture the essence of life, particularly its emotional realities. She rejected sentimentality or anything that condescended to children. Nordstrom became the model children's book editor who, while maintaining her own sense of self and authority, managed to take a backseat to the talent that she nurtured. She was also a smart businessperson who understood the marketplace and had strong instincts for what would sell and win prizes. Her editorial style is inculcated in young editors at HarperCollins to this day, and remains an important part of the company's culture, where art and commerce thrive equally, side by side.

Editors like Nordstrom are often thought of as the solitary champions of children's books, but it is the many other devoted people who work in publishing houses and contribute their talents in the process of making a book that help determine its success. Copy editors insure high standards of quality; designers and art directors think about how text and artwork integrate; production people control the quality of the reproduction of the book and its manufacture. Sales and marketing people provide useful feedback on how the book will be received by the various markets—bookstores, schools, and libraries—and make certain the book reaches its intended audience.

From the time *Goodnight Moon* was published to the present day, changes in technology have affected the way books are created and produced. The books in this treasury are arranged chronologically, so that the evolution of the picture book can be shown visually. One of the most dramatic technological changes in the printing process has been in the use of inks. The first four books in this collection are printed with flat colored inks; the later books are printed with four-color process inks. We have printed the first books separately with their original inks to maintain the quality and tenor of the original printing. The color separation process, which for most of the twentieth century depended upon the artist's creation of separate pieces of artwork for each color plate of film, has also evolved dramatically. Now digitized cameras enable full-color artwork to be separated much more quickly and accurately. Typeset houses have lost much of their business due to computers, which are used to design type and position it on scans of the artwork, which are then sent to the printer. Designers can be more creative with type choices and placement through the use of computers, although many adhere to the traditions of book design established over the years. The printing and binding process has changed little over the past decades, and the end product—a beautiful book that can be read and enjoyed many times over—is essentially the same.

To choose twelve books from the astounding HarperCollins backlist was no easy task, and to aid in the decision-making process, I enlisted the help of five dedicated children's literature experts. Each person on the panel contributed valuable opinions regarding the classic status of each of the books. I am extremely grateful to each one of them for their fine and caring input:

- Caroline Ward of the Ferguson Library of Stamford, Connecticut, who provided enthusiastic support, solid feedback, and help with extension activities;
- Kate McClelland of the Perrot Library in Old Greenwich, Connecticut, who was instrumental in shaping the endnotes for each book in the collection;
- Jane Marino of the Scarsdale Public Library, New York, who helped comb the Harper backlist and whose careful suggestions for specific titles were invaluable;
- Lisa Von Drasek, librarian for the Bank Street College of Education, who provided encouragement and many creative ideas for extension activities;
- Valerie Lewis, cofounder of Hicklebee's bookstore, who provided an excellent and wide-ranging sounding board for all of the selections as well as a glowing introduction.

I am also indebted to the many fine professionals who work at HarperCollins, particularly Susan Katz, Kate Morgan Jackson, William C. Morris, Andrea Pappenheimer, Mary Faria, Annette Hughes, Kathleen Faber, Pamela Lutz, Suzanne Daghlian, Allison Devlin, Patricia Buckley, Josh Weiss, Sally Doherty, and Antonia Markiet. The challenge of designing and producing this large volume was beautifully conquered by Harriet Barton, John Vitale, Albert Cetta, Alyssa Morris, Jeanne Hogle, and Lucille Schneider. I also thank Laura Geringer for her suggestion to donate royalties to First Book. Chandler Arnold at First Book has been an enthusiastic supporter of this collection. Leonard Marcus gave a thoughtful review of the endnotes and introductory material. Julie Hittman provided immeasurable assistance.

And last, but not least, I wish to thank all of the authors and illustrators who are a part of this collection, and who have profoundly affected the lives of children through their work.

It is my hope that this collection will introduce many more children to the pleasures of books and inspire them to keep reading throughout their lives.

—*Katherine Brown Tegen*
Editor

Selected Bibliography

Bader, Barbara. *American Picturebooks from* Noah's Ark *to* The Beast Within. New York: Macmillan, 1976.

Lewis, Valerie V., and Walter M. Mayes. *Valerie & Walter's Best Books for Children: A Lively, Opinionated Guide.* New York: Avon Books, 1998.

Lipson, Eden Ross. *The* New York Times *Parent's Guide to the Best Books for Children,* Third Edition. New York: Three Rivers Press, 2000.

Marcus, Leonard S., Editor. *Dear Genius: The Letters of Ursula Nordstrom.* New York: HarperCollins, 1998.

Schulman, Janet, Editor. *The 20th Century Children's Book Treasury: Celebrated Picture Books and Stories to Read Aloud.* New York: Alfred A. Knopf, 1998.

Silvey, Anita, Editor. *Children's Books and Their Creators.* Boston: Houghton Mifflin, 1995.

Spitz, Ellen Handler. *Inside Picture Books.* New Haven: Yale University Press, 1999.

Trelease, Jim. *The Read-Aloud Handbook,* Fifth Edition. New York: Penguin Books, 2001.

Index